GETTING **STARTED**

making
metal
jewelry

GETTING **STARTED**

making
metal
jewelry

Mark Lareau

INTERWEAVE PRESS.

INTERWEAVE PRESS
Interweave Press LLC
201 East Fourth Street
Loveland, CO 80537-5655 USA
www.interweave.com

Printed in China by Asia Pacific Offset.

Library of Congress Cataloging-in-Publication Data

Lareau, Mark, 1964-
  Getting started making metal jewelry / Mark Lareau.
       p. cm.
  Includes index.
  ISBN 13: 978-1-59668-025-8
  ISBN 10: 1-59668-025-3
  1. Jewelry making. 2. Art metal-work. I. Title.
  TT212.L37 2007
  745.594'2--dc22

                                                                  2006023192

10 9 8 7 6 5 4 3 2 1

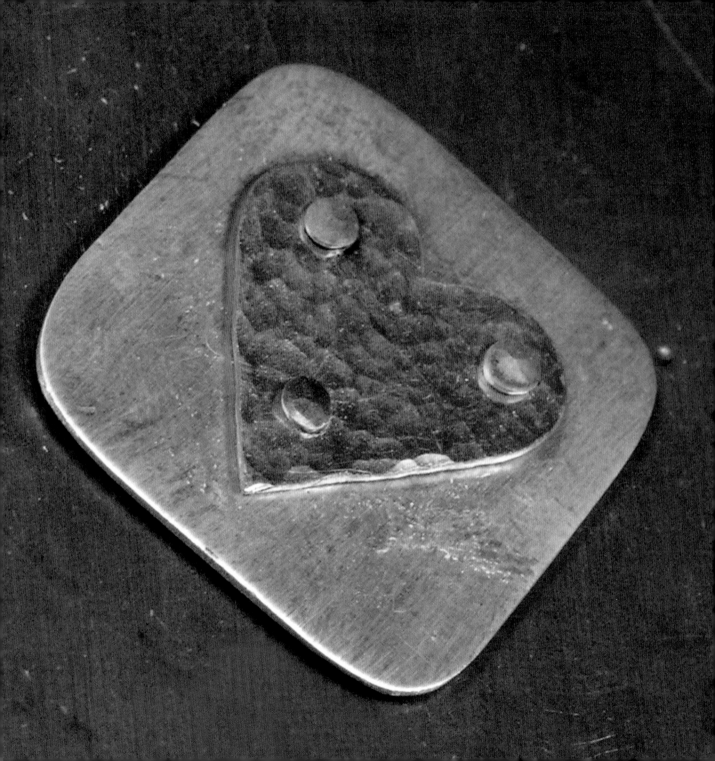

I would like to dedicate this book to my family
—Viki, Trevor, Julian, and Sophia—
who bring joy to my life every day and
who always provide such fertile fodder for inspiration
in whatever endeavor I undertake.

acknowledgments

No book is created in a vacuum. (Well, maybe when we start printing in outer space, but you know what I mean.) And this one was no different. I'd like to first thank Linda Ligon, who e-kicked me in the pants when I needed it. This is just as much her book as it is mine—I only wrote the words, the technical stuff that anyone with a little experience in the field could have provided. She tweaked, coddled, prodded, poked, and pulled it (sometimes kicking and screaming) into the wonderful tome you hold in your hands. I thought it was a fluke that Judith Durant turned the rambling mess that was my manuscript for *All Wired Up* into a terrific book; now I see that it really is the editors who deserve most of the credit.

I would like to thank Gurnd Bjordmundr, the twelfth-century Norse jeweler who invented all the techniques covered in this book. (Actually Gurnd is a literary device called an amalgam; he is actually my personification of the millions of jewelers who built upon what others did before to open up new frontiers in design, theory, and practice. Who better than a sensitive Viking jeweler to personify this?)

I would especially like to thank Tim McCreight, who taught me (besides a ton of useful technique) that it is as important to not be constrained by "rules" of technique as it is to understand and use them the way your heart asks you to. I am still not sure if that was something he was consciously trying to get across in his lessons or if it is just part of his genetic makeup, but it was one of the things I took with me, and it provided a major shift in the way I approach jewelry making. Thanks, Tim! And while I risk endless ribbing from my family and staff, I just have to say that this book would've been easier to write were it not for the people of Suramar and, specifically the wonderful folk of Not Dead Yet.

I really need to acknowledge (hence the placement in the acknowledgments) my wonderful staff at The Bead Factory. I give them grief, they give me more, I love most of them like family, 'nuff said (heh-heh). I would also be remiss in leaving out all the wonderful people who have taken classes from me at The Bead Factory (some sign up for every class, sight unseen!). You have unknowingly (well, sometimes knowingly) been my guinea pigs when I was trying out new tools (look at this new rolling mill I just bought—let's make up a class!), and I always get back at least as much from my time spent with you as you get from the classes. Thank you all.

Last, I need to say thanks again to my beautiful wife Viki, without whose gentle prodding (okay, she basically cracked the whip) there would have been no book. In fact, I shudder to think what else there wouldn't be. People often muse about what their life would've been like if they hadn't met their spouse/soulmate. I never do—it's just unimaginable to me, a life without her and our wonderful children.

contents

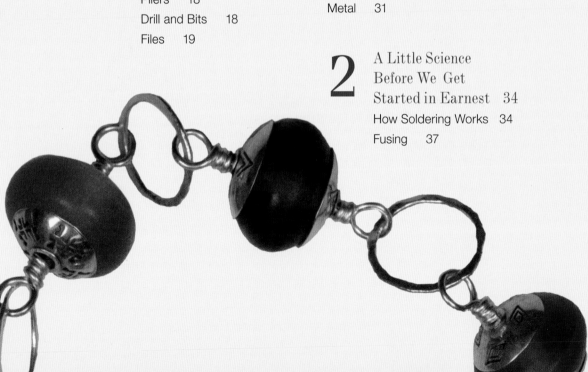

8

Mark striking metal with a chasing hammer.

introduction

Some people find the idea of metalsmithing a little intimidating. Cutting and drilling require sharp tools, sometimes even power tools. Soldering requires high heat. Chemicals are sometimes involved. But think about it. You use chemicals to clean your drains. You use a sharp motorized tool to sew a seam. Heat? Think cooking.

The fact is that the basic skills of metalsmithing are no more challenging than any number of household chores that most of us do on a daily basis. And yet mastering these basic skills—cutting, drilling, soldering, hammering, polishing—will open the door to a whole world of creative jewelry making. With these skills, if you can imagine it, you can make it.

This book is organized to help you learn your tools, develop your skills, and have a little fun along the way. I've also included some layman's explanations of the science involved. Read those parts. Understanding the basic idea of soldering is as important as understanding that baking powder makes cakes rise. Understanding your materials and processes will give you the accuracy and control to turn your visions into reality and get professional results.

Each project introduces a new idea and builds on what you've done previously. You don't have to follow them in sequence, but you'll find yourself doing less backtracking if you do. I'd encourage you to make several versions of each piece as you go along, too. It will stimulate your creativity and hone your skills as you go. Most of all, though, relax, enjoy.

Tools and Materials

Metalsmithing is a fairly gear-intensive undertaking, but don't panic! Some of the common tools you'll need are available at any good hardware store, and all of the jewelry-specific tools can be had relatively inexpensively from a good jeweler's supply provider. You'll find a few supplier suggestions in the resources section on page 105.

A few of the items you'll need will be used in every project in this book; these constitute your basic workbench and should be in place whenever you start a project. These are marked in the following discussion with a **. Some of these are consumables—you should have a decent supply so you won't run out at an awkward time. Some tools described in this chapter will be used for many projects, but not all. I've marked these with a *. The "miscellaneous" category lists small items that you should always have at hand—markers, pencils, scissors, and so forth. The basic setup—those starred items—will cost something like $100 to $200, as of the writing of this book, and they will be essential for all the fabulous works you will undoubtedly create as you go along and build your skills. You can add other tools as the need arises—letter punches, dapping block, and so forth. You might only use them occasionally, but they open some creative doors.

Finally, you'll need materials. Sheet metals, wire, solder, flux. You'll find these described here as well, and each project will list the particular materials you'll need to make it.

During the course of your jewelry-making endeavors, you will be doing lots of things that will potentially cause small shards of metal to go flying through the air. You really need to have **a good pair of safety glasses** before doing any of the projects in this book. Luckily, you can get these fairly inexpensively at any hardware store or jeweler's supply. Remember what your mom always said: "It's all fun and games until somebody loses an eye!"

The jeweler's bench pin is one of the most important tools you will need. Many metalworking techniques require you to be able to work on your piece from many different angles, and working on a table won't allow this.

A bench pin sticks out from the table it's clamped to, giving you a flat, sturdy wooden surface that offers access to almost all sides of the piece you're working on. Unless you have a jeweler's bench, which has slots along the front edge to insert the bench pin into, I recommend the kind shown here that has a bench block assembly that clamps onto a table. The block is solid steel, so you can hammer metal pieces on it.

A bench pin is usually unfinished when you buy it—just a rectangular piece of wood, beveled on one side to give it a wedgelike shape such as the one shown here. You will have to customize the shape according to your own requirements. The most common shape, and the one I recommend for its versatility, is the "V-slot," shown here as well. This is a very functional arrangement because it allows you to hold flat sheets of metal down securely on the pin while sawing inside the V. You can use a woodworking coping saw, jigsaw, or saber saw to cut the V.

**SAFETY GLASSES

**BENCH PIN

Bench pin

**RING CLAMP

Ring clamp

A ring clamp is an ingeniously low-tech device that lets you hold very firmly onto small pieces that would be impossible to hold in your fingers. A must-have. Don't even think about questioning this one. Just get it—you won't regret it!

*SAW AND SAW BLADES

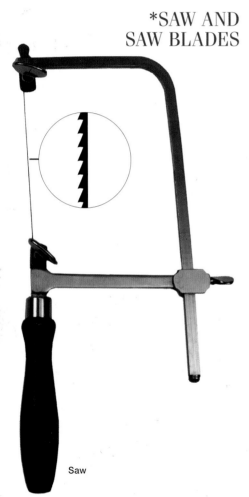

Saw

A jeweler's saw looks very much like a woodworker's coping saw, but with a much narrower and finer blade. The length of the saw frame is adjustable to accommodate different lengths of saw blades. (Most manufacturers make their saw blades pretty similar in length, but some don't.) The saw blade is held in the saw frame by two metal pads that are tightened with thumbscrews. The saw blades are fairly delicate, and they must be taut in the frame when you are sawing because a loose blade will make sawing much more difficult and will be subject to buckling and breaking.

The teeth in most standard saw blades extend from the blade at an angle. It's important to string your saw blade with the teeth angled away from the frame and toward the handle. This way, the teeth will only "chew" as you are pulling the saw down (which helps pull the metal flat against the bench pin).

Saw blades are available in different sizes based primarily on the number of teeth per inch. Generally, the more teeth per inch, the finer and cleaner the cut you can make. Coarser blades cut faster, but less cleanly.

I generally recommend using as big a blade as feasible, since you'll be refining and smoothing the sawn edges after they're cut, anyway. Don't stress out too much over the size of your saw blades—2/0 blades will work well for 22- and 20-gauge sheet metal, which you'll be using for most of the projects in this book.

Step 1

Step 2

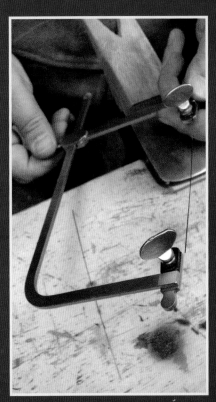

Step 3

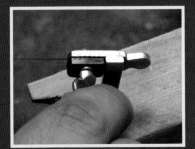

Step 4

Stringing Your Saw

Step 1. String the saw blade between the metal pad and the frame at the end closest to the handle. Make sure that as much of the blade as possible is being held between the pad and frame.

Step 2. Adjust the length of the saw frame so that the blade extends only halfway onto the pad at the other end of the frame. Tighten the thumbscrew that holds the tang in place so that length of the frame is fixed. You only really have to do this once, as all your saw blades will be the same length.

Step 3. Hold the saw handle in your dominant hand and place the end of the saw frame into your bench pin. Push the handle in toward the bench pin so you are slightly bending the frame until the saw blade extends as far into the pad as possible.

Step 4. While you have the frame bent, tighten the thumbscrew at the end of the frame that is in your bench pin.

Step 5. When you take the saw out of the bench pin, the frame will "unbend" and pull the saw blade taut. If you've done it correctly, you should hear a "ping" like a violin playing pizzicato when you pluck the blade.

Step 5

**METAL SHEARS OR TIN SNIPS

Metal shears

A good pair of metal shears, which are relatively inexpensive, will cut sheet metal into smaller, more manageable sizes. The only problem with them is they don't really cut the metal so much as "rip" it, with one side of the snips pushing down on the metal and the other side pushing up, tearing it apart. The resulting stresses often warp the metal so you have to flatten it for use afterwards (see the discussion below on hammers, specifically rawhide or plastic mallets). It is also really hard to make a cut straight if it's longer than the length of the cutting blade. Although prohibitively expensive to all but the most dedicated hobbyist or professional, a guillotine shear will create perfect, straight cuts without warping the metal. You can put that on your wish list for the future.

HAMMERS

I have a number of different hammers, each one perfectly suited to the task I set it to. While you can use some of these hammers to do several different things, I recommend getting at least one of each of the hammers listed here for the projects in this book. At the very least, you should have the ball-peen hammer and mallet.

*Ball-peen hammer.** This is a good all-purpose hammer. The wide (peen) side is great for flattening wire (but not so good on sheet metal). The ball side can be used repeatedly to create a nice "hammered" look to your pieces.

Chasing hammer

*Chasing hammer.** This hammer is used for hitting other tools such as punches or stamps. Different-shaped chasing tools are struck with the hammer, making indentations that can be arranged in patterns in the metal. The wide, flat face of the chasing hammer is perfect for this, and the ball side is often smaller than the ones usually seen on ball-peen hammers. The distinctive handle is nice and wide at the far end because often you are striking the chasing tools repeatedly for long periods of time, and a wide, form-fitting handle causes less hand cramping.

Riveting hammer

*Riveting hammer. This small hammer is used to form rivets. There'll be much more about the function of the riveting hammer when we get to the riveting project on page 75 (by which I don't mean to suggest that the other chapters aren't exciting, just that we will be making and using rivets).

*Rawhide and/or plastic mallet. These are usually used to shape metal onto a form without crushing the metal itself. The form can be a ring or bracelet mandrel to get a nice even curve, or a flat bench block to flatten a piece that has been accidentally bent.

The difference between a rawhide and plastic mallet (besides cost) is mostly in the "bounce" you'll get off them when they hit something. Most plastic mallets are made of a tough nylon, which will harden and form metal, but won't crush or flatten it. When you hit something with the plastic mallet, it usually bounces away from your work pretty quickly. A rawhide mallet is made of a strip of rawhide that is rolled up and often soaked in shellac for enhanced durability. When you strike whatever you are working on with it, the hammer doesn't bounce back like the plastic mallet will.

TIP: Here are a couple of hammering tips.
First, always hold the hammer as far down the handle as you comfortably can. The closer you are to the hammer head, the more likely you will be to hit your fingers (I know that seems counter-intuitive, but trust me). Second, when you are hammering with a steel hammer against a piece of metal, be aware that you are essentially transferring the image from the surface of the hammer to the surface of the metal. If the face of your hammer is nice and smooth, so will be the flattened part of your metal. If the face is blemished and pitted, so will be the surface of the metal be after you've hammered it.

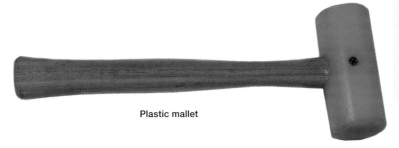

Plastic mallet

*PLIERS

Any project that involves wire—jump rings, chain, little findings, embellishments—will require pliers. You'll need flush-cutter pliers for, obviously, cutting wire. You'll need round-nose and/or chain-nose pliers for shaping wire.

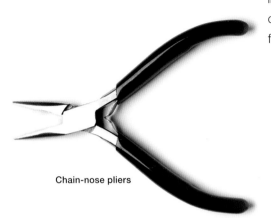

Chain-nose pliers

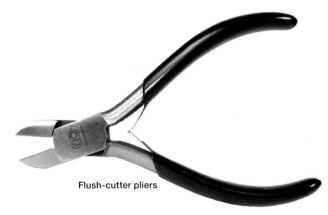

Flush-cutter pliers

*DRILL AND BITS

At some point, probably sooner rather than later, you will need to be able to drill holes in your pieces. Whether you need the holes to dangle things from them or to string a saw blade through to make a cut-out portion, the end requirement is basically the same.

A small handheld rotary tool such as a Dremel or flex-shaft kit will work great for making jewelry. The drill bits should be ones that are specifically made to cut metal (check the packaging at the hardware store before you buy!). Get several assorted sizes and get extras of the smallest ones. Don't stress out over what size your drill bits are unless you need one specifically for a certain project (such as the rivets on page 75). You should have a "drill board" handy to drill your pieces on (I use an inexpensive kitchen cutting board). Use something

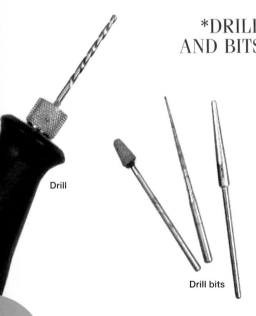

Drill

Drill bits

that you won't mind eventually throwing away, because every time you drill a hole in your metal pieces, you'll be putting another hole in the board!

*Center punch This minor but essential tool, which you can buy at any hardware store, is critical for drilling holes in metal accurately.

Half-round, needle, and key files Files come in myriad sizes and shapes and are used to remove small amounts of metal from whatever they rub up against. File teeth are formed by making many small cross-hatch cuts in the steel, creating small teeth between the intersections.

The teeth in a file are angled out toward the tip of the file and only "chew" on the metal as you push in one direction. It is important to keep your files clean so they will perform at peak efficiency. When you notice bits of metal debris clogging the teeth, simply clean them out by pulling a wire brush across the surface of the file in the same direction of the "cuts."

A good file will last forever if you take care of it. Full-size files are generally sold without a handle, though handles can be purchased separately. Smaller key files usually do have handles, and the smallest needle files don't use handles at all. For most of the projects in this book you will need only a good half-round file and a set of needle files.

*FILES

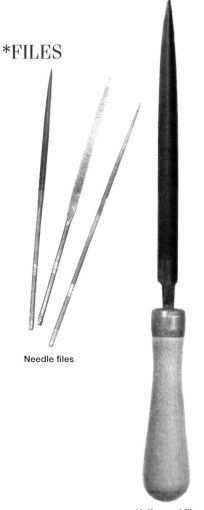

Needle files

Half-round file

How Polishing Papers Work

When you rub polishing paper over metal, you are essentially creating many small scratches in the surface. The deepest channels are the depth of the biggest pieces of polishing medium. (For purposes of explanation, let's call these valleys thirty microns deep.) If you were to look at a cross section of the metal, you would see the many steep peaks and valleys that you've created with your paper. Light that bounces off the surface of the metal doesn't bounce straight back off the surface, but bounces off the sides of the steep peaks at various sharp angles, creating a diffused (or "brushed") look.

Imagine now that next you use a paper with finer grit (say fifteen microns). If you polish with the finer paper until all the peaks have been "scraped down" so the valleys are only as deep as this paper can make (fifteen microns), the light bouncing off the peaks will bounce off at less sharp an angle, and will therefore seem less diffuse.

Each time you switch to a finer paper, you should, whenever possible, polish perpendicular to the previous "scratches" until all the previous scratches are gone. This way you will be sure that all the "valleys" are only as deep as the paper you are currently using. If you keep doing this with finer and finer papers, you could conceivably reach a point where the valleys are as little as 1 micron deep. Light will now bounce almost straight back off the surface of the metal, giving it an almost mirrorlike finish!

Pretty much everything you make with metal will need to be polished on all visible surfaces to some degree. Small gouges, blemishes, pen marks, etc., in the surface of the metal are unsightly, and you'll want to get rid of them. In addition to the polishing papers and cloths described next, I always keep a good supply of emery boards and fingernail buffers on hand. The ultimate polishing tool is the electric tumbler, a drum partially filled with fine steel burnishing shot of various shapes and sizes specifically designed for this purpose. It can handle several pieces at once, but it is expensive and beyond the scope of this book.

**POLISHING AND FINISHING MATERIALS

3M polishing papers

Rubber polishing block with work in progress.

Sandpapers, polishing papers, and the like work by removing material from the surface of the metal. Polishing papers have grit numbers (often printed on the back) based on the size of the largest pieces of polishing medium stuck to the surface of the paper.

The 3M Company has elevated the science of polishing papers to perfection, in my opinion. It has created a series whose media are all exactly the same size for each grade of paper. Papers are available in a set of six. The coarsest has grit particles thirty microns in diameter (a human hair is about 100 to 150 microns) down to the finest, whose grit is an infinitesimal one micron (that's one millionth of a meter!).

Chemically infused polishing cloths are not meant to be used to make rough surfaces smooth but to make them more reflective. These are usually soft chamois or felt material with a polishing chemical embedded in them. Where the abrasives above polish metal using their subractive properties (they remove the "peaks"), these make use of the chemical's additive abilities to "fill in" very tiny scratches so light isn't diffused by them, making the surface appear flawless.

**RUBBER POLISHING BLOCK

There is nothing more frustrating than trying to polish a small piece of metal that keeps shifting around your workspace. A polishing block is just a vulcanized rubber cube that will grip small pieces placed on it for easy polishing.

Mark rubbing polishing paper over metal.

*TORCH AND SOLDERING TOOLS AND MATERIALS

For small soldering jobs (like soldering jump rings closed or soldering posts to earrings), a small butane torch such as the one you use for your crème brulée (if you go in for that kind of thing) will probably work just fine. For larger jobs, like "sweat soldering" cut-metal shapes together or soldering bezels, a larger acetylene/atmosphere torch will make the job easier, as the flame is larger and a little hotter than the small butane torch (although the small torch will still work in many cases). Always follow the manufacturer's directions when lighting a torch and be aware of local safety regulations regarding the storage of compressed gas cylinders.

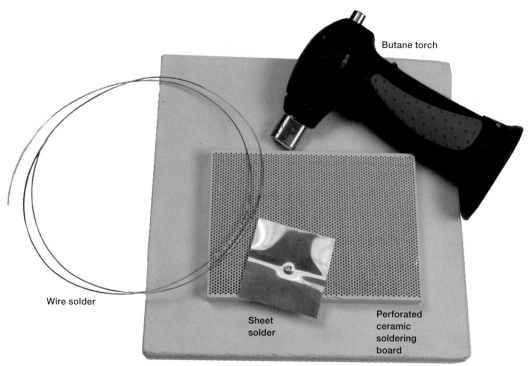

Butane torch

Wire solder

Sheet solder

Perforated ceramic soldering board

Heat-proof tile

*Soldering surface. You'll need a fireproof surface to do your soldering on. Ceramic boards work well because they act as a bit of a "heat sink," actually pulling heat away from the surface. This is advantageous for soldering small parts because it lets you adjust heat build-up quickly. This will begin to make sense when you do it.

*Flux. Flux absorbs oxygen, which will bond with copper (which is present in sterling silver, brass, copper, and gold that is not 24k) to create copper oxides on the surface of your piece. The temperatures required for soldering will significantly speed up this process. You will need some chemical agent that will create a more attractive place for the oxygen to go to than onto the copper, and this is where flux comes into play. Apply a little bit of flux where you are going to solder, and the dreaded copper oxides (which will make your piece "dirty," prohibiting the soldering process) won't be readily able to form.

Of all the fluxes I've tried, I like the Handy Flux brand best. The white paste can be thinned with water, it brushes on easily, and it very consistently turns clear exactly at 1100 degrees Fahrenheit (which is very useful when you are trying to gauge how hot your work is getting).

Beware though, fluxes (and the fumes they give off when you're working with them) are fabulously poisonous. Be sure to wash your hands after playing with them and use only in a well-ventilated area.

*Soldering pick. Used for picking up molten spheres of solder and placing them right where you need them, onto the hot metal.

Soldering pick

Depletion Gilding

There's a curious chemical process called depletion gilding that happens to some alloys when you place them in pickle. Imagine your alloy as a pomegranate. (While you're at it, imagine we're using red brass, which is 70 percent copper and 30 percent zinc.) The yummy red seeds are the zinc, and the white pithy material is the copper. If you pick out all the seeds (the zinc) near the exposed surface of the pomegranate, you are left with just the white pithy material (the copper). This is exactly what happens when you put your red brass in pickle: the acid solution eats away at the zinc faster than it eats away at the copper in the alloy, and you are left with what looks like copper. You will have to abrade the surface with some polishing papers to get all the way back down to your alloy. This is not copper being added to the surface; it's zinc being depleted from the surface, hence the name.

**Tweezers. For holding pieces in a specific position while soldering or picking them up afterward when they're still hot.

**Pickle and pickle pot. For cleaning your pieces after soldering. Pickle is a weak acid solution that "unbinds" the oxygen from the copper oxides, releasing copper particulates into the pickle solution. Note that you should *never use stainless steel* tweezers, tongs, or other tools to fish your pieces out of the pickle. The chemical reaction between steel and your pickling solution will create an electrical charge, turning your pickle pot into a copper plating bath! I know what you are thinking: "Great! I love the look of copper! I'll use this curious chemical reaction to my advantage and plate some stuff!" Well, don't: It's not a pretty, shiny copper plate, it's an ugly dirty brownish gray.

**Tongs. For the reason mentioned above, you need a pair of wooden or copper tongs.

*Solder (See page 34 for an in-depth discussion of solder.) Pronounced: sodder, not SoL-der (the "L" is silent). We'll be using thin sheets of solder rather than the fat wire-type solder used by plumbers and electricians.

Note that you should never use stainless steel tweezers, tongs, or other tools to fish your pieces out of the pickle.

Cross-lock tweezers

DAPPING BLOCK

A dapping block is a solid metal cube with hemispherical depressions in various sizes. Place a piece of sheet metal (often cut into a circle) over the depression, strike it with the corresponding punch (which should fit it perfectly), and you get a cupped shape or dome. You can even make matching domes and solder them together to make spherical beads!

PATTERN PUNCHES

Metal design punches are used to transfer an image onto a piece of metal by placing the face of the punch on the surface of the metal and striking the other end with a chasing hammer. Punches are "reverse negatives" of the desired shape since the depression they make in the metal surface is the mirror image of the punch. This is really noticeable only with letter punches.

MANDRELS— RING AND BRACELET

Bracelet mandrel

Ring mandrel

A ring mandrel is both a measuring and a shaping tool in one. Plastic and wood ones are fine for measuring, but I heartily recommend getting a steel one for shaping. (We are going to be bashing this thing with a mallet!)

Bracelet mandrels are pretty much identical to ring mandrels, only way bigger! They are generally available round (for bangle-type bracelets), or oval (for cuff-type bracelets). Either kind will work (more or less) for the projects here, although as you make more jewelry, you'll probably want one of each. (You can "make do" with a wooden rolling pin, baseball bat, or some such, but a real mandrel is a nice tool to have.)

Mark using riveting hammer.

Getting Started Making Metal Jewelry

*LIVER OF SULFUR

Liver of sulfur is an antiquing agent of sulfurated potash (potassium sulfide) that will create a patina on your work. It's available in liquid form or in raw chunks that you'll have to mix yourself. (I much prefer the raw chunks, as they tend to have a longer shelf life.)

The best way to prepare it is to pour some very hot (not boiling) water into a small dish and throw a smallish chunk or two into it. (You wanted exact weights and measurements? Sorry, think of this as gourmet cooking, the subtleties of intuition making the difference between a supremely delicious dish and disaster. Don't worry, you can't mess it up too badly. Just do it.) The perfect solution has a somewhat yellow-ish tint to it, about like lemon-lime Gatorade.

Oh yes—it stinks. I mean really stinks, so much that some people become nauseated from the odor. While the fumes are not toxic, it still may be a good idea to do this outside or with excellent ventilation.

**MISCELLANEOUS ITEMS

From time to time you'll need all of the obvious: pencils, markers, ruler, scissors, label paper for transferring an image onto metal. A particularly useful tool that is not so obvious is the divider. This looks basically like the kind of compass mathematicians use when doing geometric computations, except both sides have points that can be used to scrape a perfect circle into sheet metal. Very handy when you are making circles like the ones we'll be needing for the caps in the project on page 66.

Divider

Most of the projects in this book use readily available and relatively inexpensive materials. Once you've got a good grip on the basic skills you can go forth and buy whatever exotic metals in whatever wacky gauges you can get your hands on.

For learning purposes, though, I suggest getting some 22-gauge (or even 20-gauge) sheet metal in copper, brass, and sterling silver. We'll use the copper and brass to play with and learn on, and in some of the later projects (when you aren't as worried about ruining $$ worth of precious metals) we will get out the sterling. Some of the projects will use wire embellishments, and some (jump rings, chains) are actually made of wire. I'd suggest that you have on hand copper and silver wire in sizes 22, 20, and 18 gauge. I am not going to go into any but the most rudimentary wire techniques in this book, because there is an excellent reference available for all your wirework questions (*All Wired Up*, by me!).

Some metals that you will be working with (like sterling silver and brass) are alloys. An alloy is very simply a metal that is manufactured by mixing other pure elemental metals together. For example, brass is an alloy made from copper and zinc. The ratio of copper to zinc can vary wildly depending on what color of brass you want to achieve (yellow brass is around 70 percent zinc to 30 percent copper, where red brass is more like 30 percent zinc to 70 percent copper). Either way, it's still brass.

Sterling silver is also an alloy—92.5 percent silver and 7.5 percent "other." (The other is almost always mostly copper, although there is a curious alloy being marketed as "tarnish resistant" Argentium Sterling, which uses germanium as one of the constituent elements.)

METAL

Sheet metal and wire

A Little Discourse on How Metals Behave

Many of the metals you will be working with for jewelry have a crystalline structure (that is, the atoms in the molecules are arranged in a crystalline array which, in most of these metals, is called a face-centered cube). When the metal is most soft the crystals will be fairly randomly oriented, with wide spaces between their edges. As you work the metal by hammering, bending, and so forth, the crystals begin shifting into a more tightly packed orientation (with the spaces between the crystals getting smaller), and the metals thus become stiffer and more brittle.

Eventually (if you work the metal enough) the crystals will become so tightly packed, and the spaces between crystals so narrow, that there is no space left for the material to bend, and your metal will break. If you've bent a spoon (or any other piece of metal) back and forth until it breaks, that is what you were doing—"work hardening" the metal until it could no longer maintain cohesion.

Luckily, if you heat a hardened piece of metal to a certain temperature for a certain length of time (different for every metal), the crystalline structure will realign itself into that random, spaced-out orientation it had in the beginning. (Metallurgists, who, I have decided, are completely devoid of originality, call this process recrystallization, but you may have heard of it referred to as annealing.)

This is how blacksmiths are able to make the things they do: they start with a hunk of metal and hammer away on it, shaping it into whatever they are making. Eventually the metal will harden to the point that it won't be able to stretch anymore without breaking, so they stick their work into the forge to heat it up (recrystallizing and softening the metal). In the movies they pull it out of the forge and start banging on it while it's still glowing hot (because it looks so cool to do that), but in real life the metal is quenched in water and cooled before hammering resumes. Some will point out that letting the metal air-cool of its own volition will make it softer than quenching (and they'd be correct). However the difference in hardness (for most metals) is negligible, whereas the comfort level is not! This is not a blacksmithing book, though, so all this is not really important except to understand what is happening to the metal as you are working with it (be it hammering, sawing, soldering, etc.).

The hardness (or softness) of metal is called the temper. The point where the temper of the metal is most soft (say, just after recrystallization) is referred to as dead soft. Metal that is of a temper about halfway between dead soft and breaking is commonly called the blisteringly obvious: "half-hard."

Mark using blow torch to solder.

2

A Little Science Before We Get Started in Earnest

If you understand a little bit of the science behind soldering, it will be much easier to determine what is going wrong if you have difficulty later.

HOW SOLDERING WORKS

Think of a peanut butter sandwich (just follow me for a minute here). The peanut butter (solder) is sticking to the two pieces of bread (your metals), holding them together. They are, however, still two separate entities with something in between. You could pull the slices of bread apart—and the peanut butter would be stuck to them—but they would come apart relatively easily.

Think now of taking your two pieces of bread, making some more really watery bread dough, and slathering *that* in between them. Imagine now that when the watery bread dough seeps into the pores of the bread slices, you throw it all back into the oven and bake it. The watery bread dough that was in between (and indeed in the very fabric of the bread slices), has now baked, and the whole thing is one cohesive piece of bread. No slices, no peanut butter, just bread. This is exactly what you are doing when you are hard soldering.

When you think about soldering, maybe the image of hot soldering irons, gray wire solder, and a melting blob comes to mind. That's not this. Those "low temperature" solders work great for electrical applications or plumbing but have very limited use for jewelry. Earlier, we talked a bit about the crystalline structure of most metals used for jewelry. If you skipped that part, do yourself a favor and take a minute to read that now. It's on page 32.

Think of the spaces in the crystalline structure of the metals as being like the "pores" of the bread. (For all you angry metallurgists out there who are about to e-mail me—I know it's not really like that, but it makes a good visual image.) Imagine now that you have an alloy that melts at a lower temperature than the metals you are soldering together (which you do—the solder!) If you place some of that alloy (the solder) between the parts you are soldering together and heat the parts to the temperature at which the solder melts (or flows), the fluid crystals will flow into the spaces of the crystalline structure of the pieces you are soldering together. When the whole thing cools, the crystalline structures of all parts are now intertwined, essentially creating what's called a sub-molecular interstitial bond. It's like the bread, all one cohesive piece, no "slices."

Flow points

Solder is basically an alloy made mostly of the materials you are soldering together (silver solder for silver, gold solder for gold, etc). Silver solder is comprised of at least 67 percent silver and various ratios of other metals, mostly zinc, and is far and away the most commonly available solder and what I'll be focusing on for all the projects in this book.

Solders come in a variety of "flavors," the differences in them being the temperature at which they become liquid (called the flow temperature). The most common solders and their "flow points" are shown in the box on page 36. (These temperatures are approximate, as different manufacturers use different "recipes," which vary the flow points. They're all pretty close, though.)

Soldering a silver post to an earring. The blue flame has just brought the solder to its flow point.

Flow Points

Extra easy flow— 1270°F
Easy flow—1325°F
Medium flow—1360°F
Hard flow—1450°F
"I.T."—1490°F

The basic difference between all these solders is the ratio of silver to zinc used in them. Zinc flows at 786 degrees Fahrenheit (much lower than silver), and as the percentage of zinc in the alloy increases, it will melt at a lower temperature.

So why would you want the different flavors? Imagine you are making a complicated brooch where you are soldering decorative bits of metal to the front and some finding to the back. In theory, you would start with the higher temperature solder and use lower temperature solders for subsequent joints so you wouldn't have to heat the piece to the temperature required to melt the previously soldered parts. The lower temperature solders (especially extra-easy) have such a high zinc content, though, that they have a yellowish tint. The less zinc in the solder, the more silvery it will look, so I prefer using medium flow. Sterling silver begins to melt at 1640 degrees Fahrenheit, so you've got an almost 300 degrees Fahrenheit buffer zone where soldering will happen without turning your precious work into a formless blob of puddled metal!

There is one huge problem with soldering copper-bearing metals, though. And lest you think this is not much of a problem if you're soldering gold or sterling silver, for instance, think again. Sterling silver is an alloy of 92.5 percent silver and 7.5 percent "other," which is almost always copper. Brass is an alloy of copper and zinc. Any "yellow" gold that is not 24k is an alloy of gold and usually copper. And copper is usually all copper. The problem is that oxygen molecules (21 percent of the air you are breathing) love to bind to copper molecules to create cupric oxide (tarnish), and this happens quickly when the copper is heated.

Think of this cupric oxide as dirt clogging the "pores" in the metal, prohibiting the solder from flowing into it. Luckily, we have at our disposal a chemical agent that inhibits the binding of oxygen to copper, allowing the solder to flow freely. This chemical agent is called flux, and is available in a couple of different forms. I vastly prefer the white paste commonly sold as "Handy Flux," as it is 100 percent dependable and behaves exactly the same in any situation (which makes the whole soldering process much easier to manage). Soldering cannot happen if you don't have flux available. Don't even try it.

I'm not going into the "how-to" here. You'll get that later when you start making some pieces. This is important background science and good to know when you can't figure out why your soldering attempts are failing, as well as possibly providing some relief the next time you have insomnia. If you want to try some quick, simple soldering, skip ahead to page 95, where you'll find a project that includes simple soldering with jump rings.

Fusing is similar to soldering, except that you are using heat to bring metals to melting/flow temperatures to permanently join them. The biggest obvious difference is that you won't be using solder. Most beginners (and many professionals!) have discovered the ancient art of fusing by accident while trying to solder.

The basic premise of fusing is deceptively simple: heat the metals until the surfaces start to melt, become liquid, and flow into each other (Figure 1). I say deceptively simple, because the trick is to heat the pieces just to the point that the surface begins to flow (enters the liquidus range) while the interior of the pieces remain solid (not surprisingly called the solidus range). Again, like soldering, you will need to use flux if you are fusing any copper-bearing metals.

Fusing embellishments to a pendant.

Learning by Doing: Basic Metalsmithing Techniques

Relax and get comfortable with the techniques. Make several pendants, not just one. If you make a mistake, you've only lost a little time and minimal materials.

I'm going to walk you through the techniques involved in metalsmithing. In this chapter you'll learn such basics as transferring designs to sheet metal, sawing, filing, polishing, soldering (including using a blow torch), and pickling.

You'll put the knowledge you learned in Chapters 1 and 2 to use as you delve into your first project. You'll create a pendant using two different metals. Which metal you use is entirely up to you, although less expensive materials make for a less fearful first-time experience.

By the time you have finished your piece, you will have learned most of the basics you'll need to know to go on to more challenging and complicated pieces.

Simple Pendant

Tools

- Basics (see ** items, pages 13–30)
- Saw frame and saw blade
- Flat-nosed pliers
- Stencil template (optional)
- Torch, soldering board, solder, flux

Materials

- Sterling silver sheet metal, 22 gauge
- Copper sheet metal, 22 gauge
- Adhesive label paper (like address label paper, only bigger)

Getting ready. First, make sure that all your tools are available and ready. Your bench pin should be set up and your saw blade strung onto the saw frame. If you have skipped ahead and missed the part about how to string a saw blade, go back and read it now—it's on page 15.

Figure 1

Transferring designs to sheet metal. The design of your pendant will of course be totally up to you, but for the first one maybe you should try some simple geometric shapes (perhaps a rectangular background with a crescent moon foreground). The design can be drawn directly onto the metal with a scribe (a sharp pointed metal tool), or it can be drawn on a piece of white label paper that can then be stuck to the metal.

The really nice thing about doing this on label paper is you can design your pieces on your computer or download some public-domain clip art and print directly onto the label. This makes designing for freehand-drawing-challenged persons (like me) much easier. Stencil templates, such as the one I'm using here, are also a good way to get designs onto paper without resorting to rulers, compasses, and other drawing aids **(Figure 1)**. For a pendant like the one pictured, you'll need to have two separate components—the rectangle and the moon. Draw these separately so you can make them out of different metals. In our example, I am using sterling silver for the background rectangle and brass for the foreground moon.

Cut your paper-label motif out with plenty of room to spare, and stick it to the sheet metal (copper, in this case) **(Figure 2)**.

Sawing. This is a finesse technique. Too many people try to power through the sheet metal with their saws and later wonder why they've gone through so many saw blades. Hold the handle of your saw in the tips of your fingers so you don't try to push too hard. Let the teeth in your saw blade do the work.

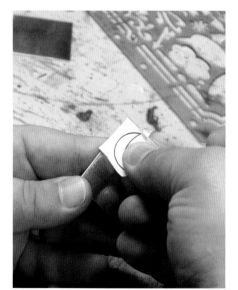
Figure 2

Probably the most important thing to remember when you are sawing is that the saw blade is creating a channel in the metal that is only as wide as the saw blade itself. Because of this, the saw blade absolutely must stay perpendicular to the sheet metal. If you shift the saw frame off the perpendicular, the saw blade will break.

Changing direction of cut. When you get to an angle and need to change the direction of your cut, you cannot just twist the saw and keep going in the new direction. The saw blade will just twist in the channel and snap. What you must do is saw in place while you gradually shift the direction of the saw blade. Think of a marching band—when they get to a street corner, the guys on the inside have to march in place as they turn until the band is ready to march in the new direction.

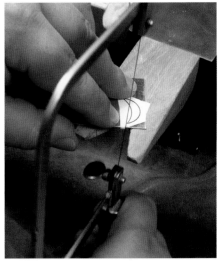

Figure 3

Place your piece of sheet metal on the bench pin and hold it securely with your nondominant hand **(Figure 3)**. Place the saw blade lightly up against the metal and begin sawing straight up and down, remembering to keep the saw blade perpendicular to the metal. I can't stress this enough. DON'T FORCE! Let the saw blade do the work of chewing through the metal, stay calm, do some zen breathing exercises or something—just remember it's finesse that makes cutting metal possible, not force.

Sawing shapes. When you are sawing out your shapes, don't try to cut exactly on the line—it's perhaps a little easier if you saw just outside the lines **(Figure 4)**. You will be refining the shapes later with a file, and it is always easier to remove metal from your work than add it (which is, while theoretically possible, way more difficult than it's worth).

Figure 4

Figure 5

Filing (refining the shape). Once you've finished sawing your crescent moon and background rectangle, you'll need to refine the shapes with your files. Hold your piece of metal in the ring clamp, arranging the side you want to file pretty close to the edge on the clamp (flat side for flattish edges, round side for roundish edges) **(Figure 5)**. Push the wedge tightly into the other end of the clamp. You don't want the metal to hang too far out the end of the clamp, or the metal might bend as you file, which will make soldering really difficult.

Hold the ring clamp in your bench pin with your hand below the bench pin and the ring clamp extending upward **(Figure 6)**. The bench pin will act as a pivot point, allowing you to get better leverage while filing.

Use an appropriate side/shape of file for the edge you are filing: flat file for flat edges or the outside of a curve, rounded file for the inside of curves. There are also myriad shapes of needle files for getting the little nooks and crannies that a standard sized file can't get into, though you won't need them for this project.

Begin filing, starting with the tip of the file on the edge, and push away from you **(Figure 7)**. (Like the saw blades, files have "teeth" that only chew when you push them in a certain direction.)

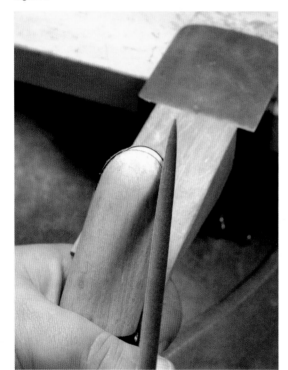

Figure 6

Getting Started Making Metal Jewelry

Repeat as necessary, changing the position of your piece in the ring clamp to afford the best position for filing.

Polishing, preparation for soldering. Now that your pieces are cut out and the shapes have been refined to perfection, it is time to prepare the pieces for soldering. There are a couple of criteria that must be met before soldering can happen: the pieces must be clean, and they must be flat (because the solder can't fill the space between the metals).

When you are cleaning pieces for soldering, avoid using polishing cloths that leave a chemical coating on the surface of the metal, because that could actually inhibit the soldering process. Use a very fine abrasive polishing paper, such as 3M brand Tri-M-ite papers, the finest of which has polishing media size of only one micron. For this piece, I used the three-micron–grit one. Place the pieces on top of a rubber polishing block to hold them in place while you polish **(Figure 8)**.

Sweat soldering! If you skipped the passages in the book that discussed the science behind soldering (page 34), go back and read them now. Understanding this background information is essential.

The soldering technique we are going to use on this project is called sweat soldering. We'll paint our pieces with flux, place a small chip of solder between our crescent moon foreground shape and the rectangle background shape, heat the pieces to the flow-point temperature of the solder, and that should do it.

Figure 7

Figure 8

Figure 9

Fluxing. Set up the background shape on the soldering board. Brush some flux on the front of the foregound piece **(Figure 9)**. Theoretically you will only need to flux the areas that are going to be soldered together, but usually it won't be a problem if you flux the whole piece. Solder will be able to flow wherever the flux is, though, so the best practice is to confine the flux roughly to the area where the two pieces touch.

Soldering a background piece. Place a small chip of sheet solder on the background piece **(Figure 10)**. How much you need will be determined by how much surface area your foreground piece will cover, but it really doesn't take very much solder to work. As I mentioned before, the solder isn't going to be filling gaps between the two pieces, so a little goes a long way. For the sample illustrated here, we'll use a single piece of solder around two millimeters square.

Adding a foreground piece. Flux the back of the foreground piece (the side that is going to be soldered to the other piece) and arrange it on the background piece according to your initial design **(Figure 11 and 12)**. Make sure that the chip of solder now between the pieces is close to the center of the foregound piece.

If the flux is really wet and "goopy," wait a few minutes until it dries. Most paste fluxes are water-diluted to make

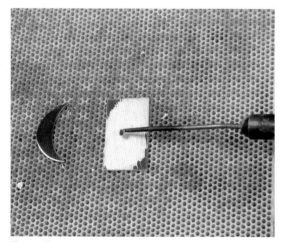

Figure 10

them easier to apply to your work, but if you heat it too quickly when it's wet, the water in the flux will start to boil, bubbling and popping on the surfaces, shifting the placement of your pieces, and even sometimes pushing the chip of solder out from under the foreground piece. You'll know the flux is dry when it turns completely white (like confectioner's sugar).

Heating up (using the torch). Light your torch and begin heating the piece evenly, moving the flame in a slow circular motion **(Figure 13).** Keep the flame within the perimeter of the piece (don't waste any of that heat), and try not to focus the flame too much on the foreground piece. The idea here is to heat the whole piece evenly so both parts reach the magic temperature (the flow point of your solder) around the same time. If you focus the heat only on the foreground, it will reach temperature first, and the solder will melt and flow into it but not into the background (because it hasn't reached flow point). Usually this isn't a problem, but you should be aware of it just in case.

You'll know when the pieces have soldered when the foreground piece settles down onto the background piece so any gaps between them have completely disappeared. Congratulations! You've just created your first sub-molecular interstitial bond!

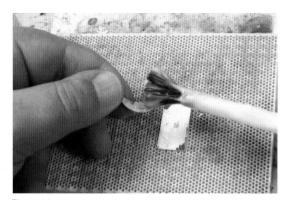

Figure 11

Figure 12

Figure 13

Figure 14

Cooling off. Quench your piece by dropping it into a dish of water. (I love the sound it makes when you do that!) **(Figure 14).**

Pickling. No matter how much flux you put on the pieces before soldering, some cupric oxides will form on the surface of the metal. Some flux may also still be clinging to the piece. In any case, it will look kind of dirty, and you may even have some weird colors going on—but don't panic! It's supposed to look this way after soldering. That's what the pickle is for. Drop your piece into the warm pickle *(remember to use copper or wood tongs for this, not steel)* and monitor its progress. If the pickle is warm, it shouldn't take more than a few minutes for the piece to become mostly clean.

Remember the bit about depletion gilding on page 26? The surface of your piece may look slightly matte, the copper may be slightly discolored, and the sterling may look somewhat "white"—but don't panic! The pieces are for all intents and purposes "clean." This is just depletion gilding at play. We'll make the pieces beautiful after we've soldered a bail to the back.

Adding a simple bail. You could of course just drill a hole near the top of your piece and hang it from a jump ring, but a bail adds a professional touch. The nice thing is, it's really easy to make one!

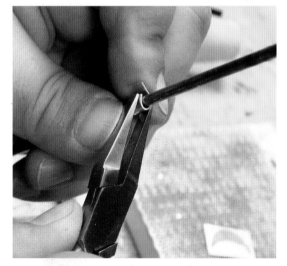

Figure 15

Saw a small rectangle (1" × ¼") out of sheet metal. File all the edges so they're perfect.

Using a steel rod, knitting needle, or something similar, pull the metal around it using a flat-nose pliers until it meets itself like a "P" **(Figure 15)**.

Solder this to the back of the piece the same way you soldered the foreground and background pieces together (remember, flux, chip of solder, torch) **(Figure 16)**.

Finishing. After you have soldered the bail to the back of your pendant and left it in the pickle pot for a few minutes, you will have to give your piece a final polish with polishing paper. This will require a bit of elbow grease! Use the three-micron grit paper.

Figure 16

Simple Earrings with French Wires or Posts

Tools

- Basics (see ** items, pages 13–30)
- Saw frame and blade
- Stencil template (optional)
- Torch, soldering board, sheet solder, flux
- Cross-lock tweezers
- Jeweler's finger guard tape (optional)
- Drill, center punch, drilling board

Materials

- Sterling silver sheet metal, 22 gauge
- Copper sheet metal, 22 gauge
- French-type earring wires
- Sterling silver earring posts

Unlike drilling a hole in wood, drilling in metal requires that you apply pressure and push. The speed of the drill bit is not as important as the pressure you apply. In fact, the high speed of the bit, without pressure placed behind it, will just heat the metal up and make it harder to hold in place.

The pendant you just made can be adapted very easily to all kinds of variations. For instance, you can make a pair of earrings by either drilling a hole (to attach a French wire), or by soldering an earring post directly to the back of the piece.

Make a couple of pairs of components like the one in the pendant project you just finished (pages 39–47), only smaller, earring-sized. Make the two pieces the same, or play around a little for an asymmetric look. Or try something completely different, such as the pair shown on the previous page.

Drilling a hole for an ear wire. To drill a hole in a piece of metal, you cannot just put the end of the drill bit against the metal and start drilling. There must be a small indentation on the surface of the metal for the drill bit to settle in. Otherwise the drill bit will tend to spin across the surface of the metal, creating an unsightly gouge across your beautiful jewelry.

Creating the indentation. Start with your piece on a steel bench block. Place a center punch tool right at the point you want to drill your hole **(Figure 1)**. Take into account the size of the drill bit (and by extension, the size of the hole) when deciding where to position your center punch, or you might end up too close to the edge and your drill hole will break the outer edge of the metal.

Once you have decided where to place the center punch, stop looking at where the punch is touching the metal. Instead, look at the top of the punch. Strike the top of the punch with your chasing hammer so you create a small indentation in the metal **(Figure 2)**.

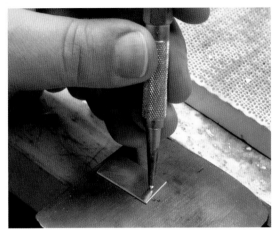

Figure 1

Figure 2

Figure 3

Figure 4

Figure 5

Drilling the hole. Set your work up on your drill board. Place the tip of your drill bit in the little indentation you just made and begin drilling your hole **(Figures 3 and 4)**. I've wrapped my fingers with jeweler's finger guard tape to better hold the metal in place, and to protect against the heat generated by the friction of the drill on metal.

Once you start drilling, you must keep a *very* secure hold on the metal. Otherwise the bit may jam in the metal, spinning it around slashing your fingers to pieces! Ouch! The friction of the drill bit on the metal will make the piece heat up.

Finishing touches. After the drill bit has made it all the way through the metal into the wood board, don't stop drilling until you have gradually backed the bit back out of the wood. If there are small burrs of metal around the hole (on either side), you can get in there with a needle file (if the hole is big enough) or with a reamer bit.

Now attach ear wires to the holes to finish your earrings **(Figure 5)**!

Soldering an earring post. Here you'll use a sterling silver earring post, available from jewelry supply companies. One end of this post has a small notch cut into it. That's the end that will go through your ear, so make sure you solder the other end to your earring.

Fluxing. Place your earring backside up on the soldering board.

Place a small spot of flux where you want the ear post to go **(Figure 1)**. Remember that (theoretically), solder will only be able to flow where you've placed flux, and this small spot of flux should keep the solder mostly in that one small area as it flows. (I say "theoretically" because in practice, the solder will often flow out past the perimeter of the spot of flux you've so carefully laid out. Another chemical agent called antiflux will very reliably prohibit the solder from flowing onto any area you've treated with it, so you may paint a circle around the spot of flux to keep the solder in a tight space. Not neccessary, but I thought it may be good for you to know that such a thing exists!)

Soldering. Cut a very small chip of solder and place it right on the spot of flux **(Figure 2)**.

Set up the notched end of the ear post in a pair of cross-lock tweezers and flux the end that will be soldered to your work. I'm going to explain what happens next in some detail because it'll all happen so quickly.

Heating. Adjust your torch so the flame is pretty narrow. Focus the flame directly onto the small spot of flux **(Figure 3)**. Remember that the flame should not leave this spot until the post is soldered!

Figure 1

Figure 2

Figure 3

Figure 4

The solder will melt first, forming a tiny sphere. (This is caused by surface tension, but you don't need to know that to succeed.)

When the area of the earring you are working on reaches the flow point of your solder, the tiny sphere of solder will spread out into a puddle **(Figure 4)**.

Placing the earring post. At this point, place the ear post on the earring precisely in the middle of the puddle. When this first happens the cold post will make a small concave "dent" in the puddle. When the post also reaches the flow temperature of the solder, you will see it actually creep up the sides of the post (this happens very quickly, almost immediately, because the post is so thin).

Once this happens you must very quickly move the flame away and (while still holding the post into the back of your earring) give the solder a second or two to cool. That's all there is to it **(Figure 5)**!

Pickling. Pickle your piece for a few minutes, polish it, add an earring back. Make another, put them in a nice little gift box, and give them to a very appreciative friend or loved one. (My experience is that as long as you preface the opening of the box with "Look what I made you . . . ," most reasonably kind-hearted people will be very appreciative, no matter how homely the jewelry actually is.)

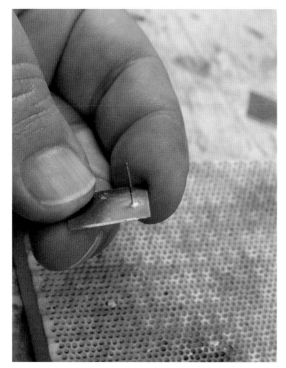

Figure 5

Getting Started Making Metal Jewelry

Simple Fused Pendant

Tools

- Basics (see ** items, pages 13–30)
- Torch, soldering board, sheet solder, flux
- Saw frame and blade
- Flush-cutter pliers

Materials

- Sterling silver sheet metal, 22 gauge
- Sterling silver scraps
- Fine silver wire, 16–18 gauge

During the course of making metalsmithing projects, you will end up with lots of little scrap pieces of silver left over from the shapes you've cut out. Don't throw these away!

Let's use some of these scrap pieces to do another project similar to the pendant above with one difference—we'll be fusing this one instead of soldering it.

Fusing, by its very nature, is an imperfect technique. If you are looking for all the components ultimately to look exactly as they do when you set them up on the soldering block, then fusing is not for you. If, on the other hand, you are willing to let serendipity (and heat) have a hand in the creation process, you will love this.

Making Little Silver Dots

Cut a few small lengths of fine silver wire, ¼" to ½", depending on how big you want your "dots" to be. Arrange them on the surface of your flat soldering board (Figure 1).

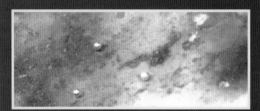

Figure 1

Put the torch on them until they melt (Figure 2). Keep the heat on them until they become so liquid that they form spheres. That's it! Quench the dots, sand off any residual ceramic that may have stuck to them, and put them aside to be used in your project.

Figure 2

Unlike soldering, you will be heating your work to the temperature at which the surfaces of the pieces actually begin to melt. Capillary force will try to pull all touching liquids together, causing them to fuse. If you keep the temperature just close enough to the melting point that the surfaces become liquid, but the interiors of the parts stay mostly solid, you can get your pieces to fuse without substantially changing their shapes. Personally, I think it's more fun to let heat have its way. Straight edges will begin to soften and warp, angular corners will begin to curl up or take on spherical shapes. Some sections may become very liquid while others stay relatively solid, allowing for some unexpected results.

Before we get started, though, I just want to take a side trip to make a few of the little pieces you can use for decoration. I love using small spheres of varying sizes when I am fusing. No good reason behind it—I just like the look of a few strategically placed "dots" on my pieces. You are going to make these using various lengths of some big (18-gauge to 16-gauge) fine silver (.999) wire. Fine silver works much better than sterling for this: when you melt an alloy like sterling, the constituent copper binds very quickly with oxygen, creating cupric oxide "hard spots" on the surface of the liquid metal. Surface tension will pull the liquid away from the surface of the molten sphere, creating unsightly blemishes in the surface that cannot be polished clean.

Cutting the background piece. Cut out a background piece. For ease of illustration, let's use a similar shape to the first pendant we made (page 39). Brush a thin layer of flux over the surface of the background. This will slow the forming of cupric oxides, which may hinder the fusing process. Arrange your scrap pieces (show a little creativity here!) on the background **(Figure 1)**. You can spend a little time making the scraps "fit" a little better if you want—it's all up to you! Make sure to put a little flux on the scrap pieces you are arranging on the surface.

Fusing. Start heating the piece **(Figure 2)**. If your piece is very large, your small butane torch may not deliver enough heat, in which case you'll need a bigger acetylene torch.

Try to heat the piece as evenly as you can, bringing it all up to temperature at about the same time. When it reaches the proper temperature (starting around 1640° Fahrenheit for sterling), the metal will begin to melt. Keep the torch on the piece until you have seen all of the surface to be fused begin to "shimmer"—you can actually see the surfaces become liquid.

How much more heating you do here will be up to you and your sense of adventure. Do you leave the pieces just as you originally arranged them? Will you let the heat begin to really melt the edges so that they begin to warp and curl? Experiment a little and find your own style.

Quenching and pickling. When you have finished fusing, let the piece cool for a few minutes before you quench it. After quenching, you can pickle, add a bail to the back (see page 46) or drill a hole, and polish the piece.

Figure 1

Figure 2

Bracelet with Letter Punch Design

Tools

- Basics (see ** items, pages 13–30)
- Letter punches
- Chasing hammer
- Saw frame and blade
- Bracelet mandrel
- Liver of sulfur

Materials

- Sterling silver rectangular wire, 6mm × 2mm

This project uses some simple letter or design punches that you can find at any of the larger jewelers' supply companies (which you'll find listed on page 105).

We'll be stamping (or punching) the design from the punches right onto the metal itself. You will need a strip of metal to form the bracelet. I used a fairly heavy (6mm × 2mm) rectangle wire, which makes a thick yet elegant bracelet, but you can use any sheet metal cut to the length and width you want for yours. The letter punches we'll be using are available in several sizes, and the design punches come in so many different shapes you would be hard pressed not to find something you'd like!

The chasing hammer. The hammer you should be using for this is called a chasing hammer. The wide, flat face of this hammer is made specifically for striking other tools, exactly what we're doing here, except we'll be using some letters to stamp out a phrase, affirmation, quip, joke, whatever.

Proper stamping technique. Do this technique only on your bench block or other thick steel surface. Trying to punch letters and patterns on a wood suface—desk, picnic table, whatever—will pretty severely warp the metal, not to mention putting lovely dents all over the table!

The trick to getting the letters punched correctly is a simple matter of getting the punches lined up exactly, perfectly perpendicular to the surface of the metal. I'm going to insist that you practice stamping on some scrap material before you try to make something you plan on showing people (trust me). Don't worry too much about placement of the letter just yet—I'll have some helpful hints for that later. Just now I want you to focus on getting a nice, clean impression.

Hold the punch with the letter side down against the metal (I know it seems obvious, but you never know!) **(Figure 1)**. When you look at the face of the punch, you are looking at a reverse image of the letter—make sure it's in the correct orientation when placing it on the metal. Double and triple check to make sure (do it now!). Now, very slowly, pivot the punch up and down with the face of the letter station-

Figure 1

ary against the metal. You will feel a very faint "tap" in the punch when the top and bottom of the letter meet the metal. This will help you figure out exactly when the punch is perfectly flat against the metal. Try it now, pivoting sideways to get it flat in that orientation **(Figure 2)**.

Proper orientation. The orientation of the punch is the linchpin in the whole technique. If the face of the punch is not perfectly flat against the metal, the resulting impression will be lopsided, with part of the letter really thick and part of it really thin (which may look cool if you are doing all of them like that on purpose, but looks really dumb when some of your letters are even and some are uneven).

Once you've got the punch placed squarely, stop looking at where the punch is touching the metal. That is not where you need to focus. You need to look at the TOP of the punch, where the hammer will strike it. This will make your striking much more accurate and save you tons of grief from glancing blows. When you are getting ready to strike the top of the punch, visualize the hammer striking the tool perfectly centered in the hammer, and immediately bouncing away from the tool.

Figure 2

Following through. (Don't!) If you ever took wood shop, they told you that when you are hammering anything, you should imagine the hammer "following through" and driving the nail right through that sorry piece of wood you were nailing. This is not even remotely like that. If you "follow through" with the hammer it will strike the punch, bounce off, and strike it again as you are "following through." This will often give you a double impression or "ghost image" of your stamp: The first impression is fine, but the second is almost always very faint and uneven. And no reasonable amount of sanding will get rid of it.

Striking it! Now go ahead and strike the top of the punch **(Figure 3)**. You don't have to hit it too hard—hard enough to get a good impression but not so hard that you are stretching or warping the sheet. Now do it several more times on your practice sheet, so you'll be confident and accurate when you make your first real piece **(Figure 4)**.

Planning and spacing. As you've probably figured out by now in all your attempts at punching, getting a good impression is vital to this kind of project. The second most important thing is getting the letters placed evenly and straight.

Figure 3

Figure 4

Spacing. If you've ever messed around with the "kerning" feature of your favorite word-processing program, you'll know that if you spaced all the letters in any word exactly evenly, they'd look kind of weird. Letters like "i" or "l" should take up less space than letters like "m" or "w." It's probably best that you don't try to space out letters exactly evenly—it just doesn't look natural. Try rather to get them spaced so that the leading edge of one letter is always the same distance away from the trailing edge of the one next to it.

Aligning. If you don't pay too much attention to the vertical alignment of your letters, the end result will look very "whimsical." (Don't get me wrong—this is a perfectly valid "look" and you may want to go for it—the more anal retentive of us who can't stand that disorderly look would do well to pay attention here.) Your best bet to getting the letters lined up properly is actually pretty easy to achieve. Just get out your Sharpie marking pen and straight edge and draw a line right through the middle of where you want your letters to go. Don't worry—the mark will go away when you polish the piece after antiquing it.

When you set your letters up to be punched, center the punch on this line. Practice getting a few letters in a row stamped nice and straight. Once you've done enough that you feel comfortable with your impressions and placing, we can move onto your actual project.

Making the bracelet. Write out the phrase you want to stamp on a piece of paper and count how many letters and spaces there are. In my example, there are twenty-six letters and spaces. Draw a line at the halfway point (in my case, thirteen letters in).

TEMPUS FUGIT │ CARITAS MANET

This will be the starting point of my letter punching. I will start from the center and work my way out to the right, then I'll go back to the center and work my way out to the left. This way I will be absolutely sure that the phrase is centered.

Figure 1

Measuring and cutting (sawing). Decide how long you want your bracelet to be by measuring your wrist with a strip of paper or measuring tape. Once you have this measurement, cut a piece of rectangle wire to size. This silver stock is too thick to cut with most kinds of cutting pliers, so you'll need to saw it.

Making a bracelet blank. Hold the wire firmly in your ring clamp with the piece you want to cut off hanging out your dominant hand side **(Figure 1)**.

Hold the ring clamp in your bench pin (hold it steady!) and carefully begin sawing the length off **(Figure 2)**. Now you have a bracelet "blank."

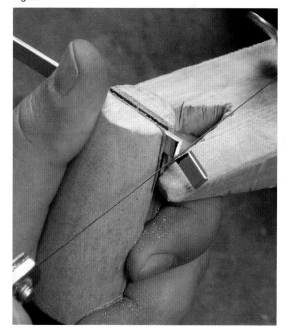
Figure 2

Figure 3

Figure 4

Details. You'll want the ends of the wire to be rounded so they don't poke into your wrist and scratch you. Holding the end of the wire in your ring clamp, file the corners into rounded ends **(Figure 3)**.

Polish the ends with your polishing papers so they are perfectly smooth.

Stamping. Now draw a line in the exact center of your bracelet blank. As explained on page 62, start from the center and begin punching out your letters **(Figure 4)**. Don't forget to double-check the orientation of the letter punches before you actually strike them with your chasing hammer! If you use

Getting Started Making Metal Jewelry

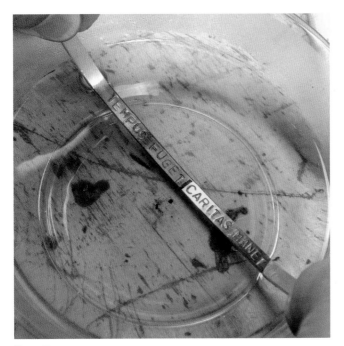

Figure 5

Figure 6

the size of bracelet blank and letter punches that I have, you won't need to draw a horizontal line down the center of the bracelet, because the punches fill the width of the bracelet.

Patina. Prepare a solution of liver of sulfur according to the instructions on page 30 and drop your bracelet into it **(Figure 5)**. This will add a very nice dark patina to the inside of the punched letters, which will remain in the crevices as you polish the surfaces with a very fine (three micron) polishing paper **(Figure 6)**.

Shaping. Hold the very center of the bracelet against the bracelet mandrel with your thumb **(Figure 7)**.

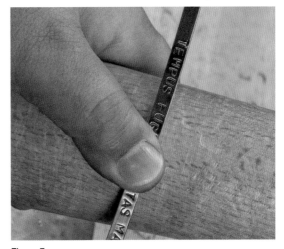

Figure 7

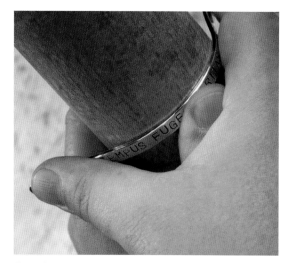

Figure 8

Pull both ends all the way around the mandrel **(Figure 8)**.

Holding the bracelet from the sides now, form the ends of the bracelet onto the mandrel with a rawhide or nylon mallet **(Figure 9)**. Admire your work **(Figure 10)**!

If you don't have a bracelet mandrel, don't despair—you can use a rolling pin, baseball bat, or other round wooden object of appropriate size. After you've shaped your bracelet into a circle, gently flatten it to conform to your wrist.

Figure 9

Figure 10

Getting Started Making Metal Jewelry

Decorative Bead Caps

Tools

- Basics (see ** items, pages 13–30)
- Dividers
- Drill, center punch, drilling board
- Decorative punches
- Chasing hammer
- Dapping block and punches
- Flush-cut pliers
- Chain-nosed pliers
- Round-nosed pliers
- Saw frame and blade
- Liver of sulfur

Materials

Sterling silver sheet metal, 22 gauge

Sterling silver wire, 18 gauge

If you do any amount of beading, you've seen them . . . gorgeous big beads with poorly formed, ugly holes. Hiding them with a bead cap is the most common way of covering up the offending blemishes. Let's take this a step further and make the caps so interesting you'll want them to be the focus of your jewelry!

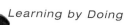

Figure 1

Figure 2

Planning the caps. First, some decisions. How wide do you want the caps to be? What kind of decoration do you want on them? How big a hole will you need in each one? Once you've decided, you can start the caps by making an indentation (like the ones we've done in preparation for drilling) where you want the hole to be.

To decide where that center hole should be, mark an X on the metal with a Sharpie marking pen **(Figure 1)**. In fact, go ahead and mark Xs for as many bead caps as you want to make. And go ahead and make an indentation in the center of each one where you'll drill a hole later.

Making perfect circles with dividers. Dividers are great tools for making perfect circles arranged around a central point. This is very important for caps because you don't want the hole to be off center! A divider works just like the compass you used in geometry class, except that both sides have sharp points instead on one side holding a pencil. Simply place one point of the divider in the center indentation and adjust the divider so the other point reaches where you want the outside edge of your cap to be. Now you can "scratch" a perfect circle in the metal, delineating your outside edge of the cap **(Figure 2)**.

Drilling holes. At this point it's probably best to drill your holes now before you cut the sheet metal into disks. Holding onto little disks of metal while trying to drill holes in them is tricky! The metal gets hot and difficult to hold onto, and if the drill bit "jams" in the metal, the disk becomes a dangerous spinning weapon.

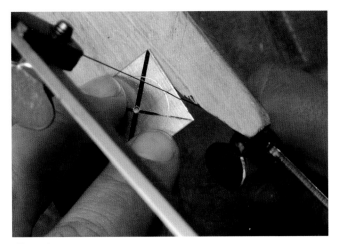

Figure 3

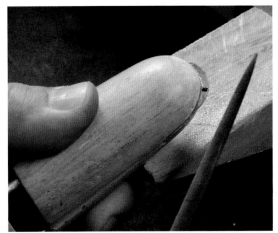

Figure 4

Figure 5

Adding designs with punches and antiquing. I know you're getting desperately anxious to cut out your bead caps—but not yet! Now is the time to add decorative punch patterns to make your caps beautifully distinctive. After punching the patterns—whatever patterns you want using whatever punches you want. Antique them in a liver of sulfur solution (see page 30) and polish with polishing papers to bring the metal back to a shine.

Cutting the caps out. Okay, now you can saw out your caps, refine the shapes with your files, make the edges beautiful, and you'll be ready to "dap" the caps into their distinctive shape **(Figures 3 and 4)**.

Dapping. Place the caps face-side down into one of the cavities of your dapping block that is larger than the cap **(Figure 5)**. The cavities are usually perfect hemispheres, so

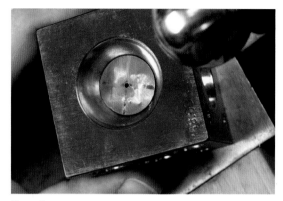

Figure 6

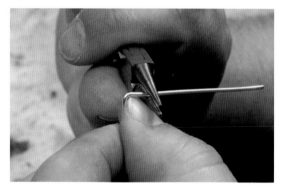

Figure 7

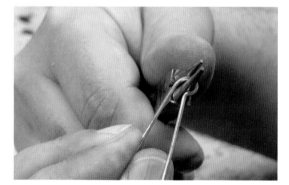

Figure 8

it won't matter where in the cavity the cap is placed—the end result will be the same (they don't have to be centered or anything). While not absolutely necessary, it's probably best to start out in a cavity that is relatively shallow so you don't try to stretch the cap too much at first, which will warp the hole. Place the corresponding dapping punch into the cavity so it rests in the cap. Using your chasing hammer, strike the dapping punch a few times, until the cap has finally assumed the shape of the bottom of the cavity. You can place your cap in subsequently smaller cavities to make the curvature of your cap deeper a little at a time **(Figure 6)**.

Capping a bead. Using flush-cutter pliers, cut a piece of 18-gauge wire about six and a half inches long. Using chain-nosed pliers, bend the first three inches over into a nice ninety-degree angle **(Figure 7)**. Think of this bend as "sacred"—you don't want to lose this bend as you work.

Now hold your round-nose pliers about ¼ inch away from the bend. Hold the wire pointing toward you and your plier-hand facing palm out. Start to loop the wire up and over by rolling the pliers away from you **(Figure 8)**. Be sure that the wire and pliers are perpendicular to each other. When you get to the point that, if you continued rolling, you'd be pulling out the sacred bend, stop rolling!

Getting Started Making Metal Jewelry

Forming a wrapped loop. Keep the round-nose pliers held in the half-loop you've just formed, but let go of the wire with your other hand. Now grasp the tail end of the wire with that hand. Continue to pull the tail onto the pliers, behind the half-loop, until the loop is completely formed and the tail end continues out perpendicular to the piece of wire the whole thing started from **(Figure 9)**.

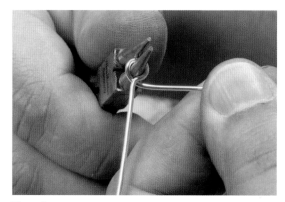
Figure 9

Holding the chain-nose pliers in your nondominant hand with the nose pointing straight out in front of you, grasp the loop with the pliers. The long piece of wire you'll be wrapping should be perpendicular to the pliers, and the tail end you pulled around the pliers to form the loop should be pointing straight out away from you. Holding the loop firmly in your pliers, begin pulling the tail end around the other end.

After you've pulled three or four wraps, snip the tail of the wire off with the flush-cutter pliers as close as you can to the shaft of wire you've been wrapping it onto **(Figure 10)**.

Figure 10

Attaching bead caps. String a bead cap, a bead, and another bead cap onto the shaft of the wire that ends in the wrapped loop. Grasp the wire near the tip of your chain-nose pliers right up against the bead cap **(Figure 11)**.

Figure 11

Figure 12

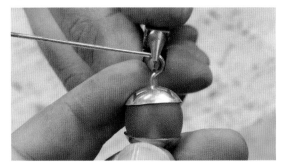

Figure 13

Figure 14

Make a nice sharp ninety-degree bend onto the top of your pliers **(Figure 12)**. Make a wrapped loop just as you did before, snipping the tail as close to the bead as you can again **(Figures 13 and 14)**. The last wrap should end up right against the capped bead.

Forming the bracelet. Assuming you have made several capped beads—enough, say, for a bracelet—you would now make another wrapped loop, string it through the next bead, and start the next wrapped loop **(Figures 15 and**

Finished bead cap

Getting Started Making Metal Jewelry

16). Stop when you've made the loop but haven't started wrapping. String the tail end of the wire of the loop you've just formed into one loop of the completed unit **(Figure 17)**. Pull it all the way on until the two loops are interconnected **(Figure 18)**. Finish wrapping the shaft up to the bead as before, snip, tweak, and you're done.

You can continue in this way, linking pieces together one at a time, until you've completed an entire piece.

Figure 16

Figure 17

Figure 18

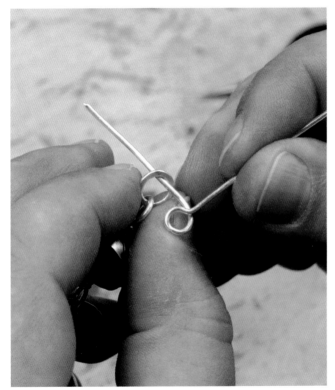

Figure 15

Textured Pendant With a Window Cutout and Dangle

Tools

- Basics (see ** items, pages 13–30)
- Drill, center punch, drilling board
- Saw frame and blade
- Ball-peen hammer

Materials

- Sheet brass, 22 gauge
- Jump rings
- Small charm or beads for dangles

To make a pendant with a cutout area, you simply drill a hole somewhere in the area that is going to be cut away so you can string your saw blade through it and saw it out. (Kind of like the old cartoons where a saw comes up from under the floor and cuts around the hero standing there . . .).

Drawing your shape and drilling your hole. Begin by drawing a shape on the sheet metal, in this case 22-gauge brass **(Figure 1)**. I've freehanded a simple circular shape with an oval off-center in it.

Use your center punch to tap an indentation in the middle of the cutout, then drill a hole **(Figures 2 and 3)**. When you've got your hole drilled, simply undo the thumbscrew that's holding your saw blade onto the frame at the point furthest from your handle **(Figure 4)**.

Figure 2

Figure 3

Figure 4

Figure 1

Figure 5

Sawing the cutout. String your saw blade through the hole, put the blade back in, tighten it, and you're ready to saw the cutout **(Figure 5).** Once you've completed the cutout, you can begin cutting the outside shape of your pendant. Don't forget to file all edges to refine your shape and make all the edges beautiful **(Figure 6)**.

Next, drill all the remaining holes. You'll need one to dangle something in the "window," and another to hang a jump ring on to string chain through.

Finishing touches. Add some texture to the surface by hammering with the ball side of your ball-peen hammer. Frequent, light taps will yield a very pleasing "mottled" surface look **(Figure 7)**.

I've dangled a tiny copper heart-shaped charm in the cutout (charming!) with a small jump ring, and placed another larger jump ring at the top of the pendant so it can be hung from a chain or ribbon. So simple, and no two alike!

Figure 6

Figure 7

Pendant with Rivets

Tools
- Basics (see ** items, pages 13–30)
- Riveting hammer (or ball-peen hammer)
- Saw frame and blade
- Drill, center punch, drilling board
- Flush-cutter pliers
- Flat-nose or chain-nose pliers

Materials
- Sterling silver sheet metal, 22 gauge
- Copper sheet metal, 22 gauge
- Sterling silver wire, 18 gauge

Riveting is a connecting technique that uses (not surprisingly) rivets to bind pieces of metal together. The technique is fairly simple and doesn't require you to buy special rivets (although you can feel free to—they are available in myriad styles). It also allows you to fasten pieces together without soldering. The technique I show you here uses some sterling silver wire to make your own rivets (a much less expensive solution).

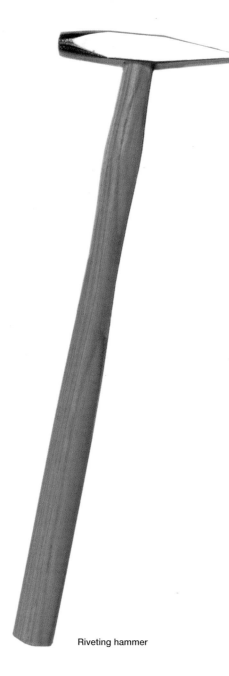

Riveting hammer

If you didn't make the first pendant in the book (page 39), go back and read the cutting and shaping instructions. This is all the same, up to adhering the foreground motif to the background. Cut out the foreground and background pieces of your project (in the case of the one pictured, a sterling silver square for the background, and a copper heart for the foreground). File and dress the edges—make them beautiful!

Riveting hammer. A piece of equipment that, while not essential, will help make this job easier is a riveting hammer. Riveting hammers are generally small, light hammers with a small, round striking surface at one end, and a wider, flat striking surface at the other. The fact that they are light make them perfect for the task we are setting them to—forming a rivet head should feel more like sculpting than nailing. Many frequent, light taps can turn a plain old piece of wire into a beautiful yet functional component of your jewelry.

Using rivets. There are a couple of things you must consider when using rivets (be they short lengths of wire such as we are using here, or commercially made rivets).

First, the hole size has to be only just big enough for the rivet to go through. The rivet has to be able to "splay" out over the edges of the hole when struck with your riveting hammer, and if the holes are too big the rivet will either buckle and bend in the hole, or just flatten out to fill the hole without securing the outer edges.

Second, there is an essential order of operations you should consider when riveting. Read this through carefully and study the pictures before you start.

Making the rivets. The rivets we are going to make are actually just short lengths of sterling silver wire that matches the size of the holes we drilled.

Cut a short length of wire (half an inch or so is plenty). Grasp this wire firmly in a pair of flat- or chain-nose pliers, leaving only a few millimeters of wire poking out the side. Hold the pliers down against the edge of your worktable so the "other" end of wire poking out your pliers doesn't get all bent up.

Drilling the foreground piece. Once you've decided where the rivets are going to go, you can drill all the holes for them in *only one* of the pieces to be riveted together **(Figure 1)**. For clarity of explanation (and because the example pictured is done this way), let's call this the foreground piece.

You can then place the foreground piece on the background and mark where *only one* of the holes will go **(Figure 2)**. Drill *only this* **(Figure 3)** hole and make a rivet in this first pair of holes.

Figure 1

Figure 2

Figure 3

Figure 4

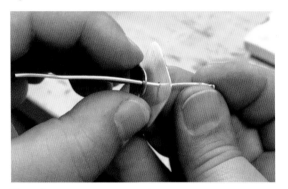

Figure 5

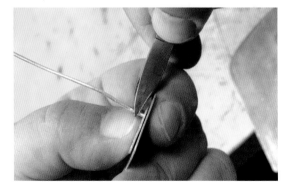

Figure 6

Drilling the background piece. Now you can drill the second hole in the background piece. Do this by drilling right through the matching hole in the foreground piece, which is now anchored in place by the rivet you just made. Complete your second rivet through this second set of holes.

Now you can drill every other hole in the background without the problem of the foreground piece "shifting," which precludes the possibilty of the holes lining up. (In our example there is only one other rivet, but if you had ten more you could drill them all now!).

Using your riveting hammer, begin flattening out one end of the wire **(Figure 4)**. This is best done by using many light, quick taps, instead of trying to muscle it. The wire may slip down into the pliers, in which case keep adjusting it in the pliers until you get a nicely splayed "head" on the end of the wire. This is best accomplished by rotating the direction of your tapping all around the end of the wire.

String the wire through the piece, back to front, so the wire now pokes out the front, with the rivet head you just made up against the back **(Figure 5)**.

The wire. Using a good pair of flush-cutter pliers, snip the wire down so only a few millimeters stick out through the foreground piece **(Figures 6 and 7)**. How much wire you

Figure 7

Figure 8

leave will ultimately determine how much of a rivet head you will be left with. You must be careful not to leave too much wire, lest the rivet be an ugly bent piece of wire. Conversely, you can't leave too little wire, or it may not splay out enough to completely cover the hole and hold the pieces securely together.

You should spend a little more time making this rivet head more aesthetically pleasing than the one you made for the back. Spend some time lightly tapping the rivet from every angle so you get a nice, even round splaying **(Figure 8)**.

Now you can place your second rivet. Only after you have placed the first two rivets can you drill the rest of the holes **(Figure 9)**!

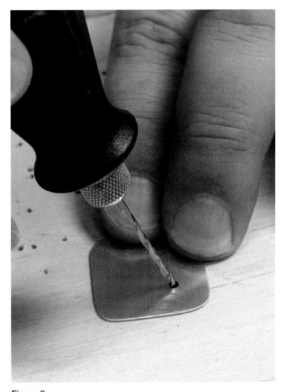

Figure 9

Two Simple Rings

Tools

- Basics (see ** items, pages 13–30)
- Saw frame and blade
- Torch, soldering board, sheet solder, flux
- Flat-nosed and/or ring-forming pliers
- Ring mandrel
- Nylon or rawhide mallet

Materials

- Low dome wire for low dome wire ring
- Sheet sterling silver, 22 gauge, and sheet copper, 22 gauge, for sheet metal ring

Making rings is a deceptively simple affair, the basic premise being that you take a strip of metal, bend it into a circle, solder, clean, polish and hey, presto! A ring is made. The two I show here give you the basis for every kind of variation you can think of.

Low dome wire ring. Low dome wire makes great rings. It's flat on one side and slightly rounded on the other. Just about every plain wedding band is made from it, so the shape is immediately recognizable.

Ring sizing vs length of blank. What size your ring ends up is wholly dependant on how long a piece of low dome wire you cut. So what length of wire do you cut? Many ring mandrels have length guides etched into them, and these are a good place to start (especially if you are making rings out of relatively thin sheet metal like the next ring we'll make).

There is one problem with bending thicker metal into a loop though—the inside diameter of the loop actually "compresses" as you bend it, making the ring smaller than you originally intended.

Luckily, there is a simple mathematical formula you can use to eliminate the shrinking problem: just add the thickness of your metal times *pi* (around 3.1416, but to make it easy we can just round down to three) to the base number listed here. The math may sound scary, but it couldn't be simpler. If your metal is, say, 2mm, multiply that times three—6mm, and add that to the length. Your calculator will do it in a jiffy.

Ring Sizing Chart

Ring Size	Blank Length
4	46.5mm
5	49mm
6	51.5mm
7	54mm
8	56.5mm
9	60mm
10	61.5mm
11	64mm
12	67mm

To get the inside diameter, be sure to multiply your metal's thicknesss by 3.14, then add it to the length.

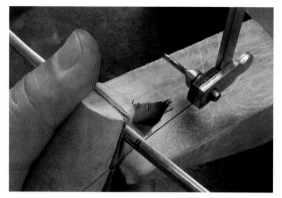

Figure 1

Figure 2

Figure 3

Most low dome wire is too thick to cut with regular jeweler's wire cutters, even if you had any, so I recommend sawing the wire to length.

Hold the wire in your ring clamp, and hold your ring clamp firmly in your bench pin. Saw your wire just slightly longer that you ultimately want it to be **(Figure 1)**.

Still in your ring clamp, file the ends to the correct length **(Figure 2)**. It is of paramount importance that the ends are perfectly squared with the sides, otherwise they won't meet flush when the ends meet, and your ring will be slightly "wonky."

Forming. When you begin forming the ring, you don't really have to make it perfectly round at all—you just have to get the ends to meet flush so you can solder them together. This job is made easier if you have a pair of pliers specifically designed for the job, called, not surprisingly, "ring-forming pliers." These are basically a flat-nose plier on one nose and a roundish oval-nose plier on the other. You can actually make your own if you have an extra pair of flat-nose pliers (which are usually easier to find, anyway), by filing down the edges of one nose until they are curved. However, I'm using my regular flat-nose pliers here, and you can do the same. Grasping one end of the wire, begin pulling the metal into a loop **(Figure 3)**. Once you've got about a third of the loop formed, grab the other end and start bending that side in.

Getting Started Making Metal Jewelry

Figure 4

Pushing. (Figure 4). In fact, let them go *past* each other so their natural resting state is to overlap a little. Then, when you pull them open to get them to meet flush, there will be sufficient tension on the ends so they push against each other. This is very important, because besides needing to meet flush, they *absolutely have to be touching!* The solder cannot fill space between the ends, so even if there is a thin gap between the ends the soldering will fail. (To be fair, I should say that as long as there is *some* area along the joint where they are meeting, the soldering may still work. The more contact there is, though, the sounder the joint.)

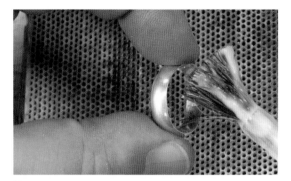

Figure 5

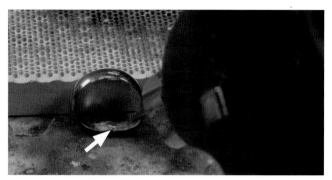

Figure 6

Figure 7

Soldering. Dab some flux all around the joint to be soldered **(Figure 5)**.

Set your ring blank up on your soldering boards as shown.

Place a small (2mm × 2mm) chip of sheet solder on the joint **(Figure 6)**. Begin heating the ring evenly with your torch **(Figure 7)**. Make sure both sides of the joint reach soldering temperature (1360° Fahrenheit for medium silver solder) at the same time; otherwise the solder may begin only flowing up one side (the "hot" side) of the ring and not actually solder the joint together.

Once soldered, let the ring cool a minute or so before you quench it in water. Clean off any residual flux and cupric oxide by placing the ring in some warm pickle.

Shaping the ring. Once your ring is mostly clean (don't worry about polishing yet), you can (literally) knock it into shape.

Place your ring on your ring mandrel **(Figure 8)**. Using a plastic mallet, begin hammering the ring on the mandrel until it is completely round. This will also harden the metal, which has been softened by the soldering process.

Polishing. Now make the ring beautiful. First, carefully file the inside of the ring on the soldering joint, using the rounded side of your file.

Using one of your coarser polishing papers, begin polishing the soldered joint on the outside of the ring **(Figure 9)**. You probably shouldn't use the coarser papers on the rest of the ring. After you get the joint smoothed up, go over the whole ring, inside and out, with the finest papers.

To polish the inside, wrap strips of polishing paper around the split bit that comes with your rotary tool **(Figure 10)**. Simply hold onto the ring and polish around the inside with sequentially finer papers until shiny **(Figure 11)**.

Figure 9

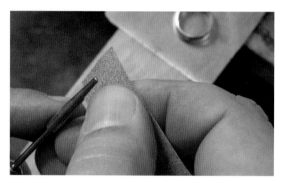

Figure 10

Figure 8

Figure 11

Figure 1

Figure 2

Sheet metal ring. Here's another simple ring that applies techniques we've picked up in earlier chapters for some terrific decoration. The sample shown uses sterling silver for the band and copper for the decoration **(Figure 1)**.

You can make this ring using sheet metal for both the shank and the decoration. I've used 22-gauge silver for the base, and 22-gauge copper for the decorative motif. Using the length/ring size table (page 81) as a guide for the length, saw a strip of metal as wide as you want your ring to be. Remember that, as with the low dome wire, the ends have to perfectly square with the sides so they meet evenly when formed into a ring. File the edges smooth. Then cut out a decorative element.

Getting Started Making Metal Jewelry

Adding decoration. Next, solder the decoration to the band **(Figures 2 and 3)**. Try your best to center the decoration on the band. This will help when you solder the ring closed—the decoration will be as far away from the joint as possible. Admittedly not very far away, but every little bit helps.

Refer to the dome wire ring if you need to, because everything else is pretty much the same. Bend the ring into a rough overlapping circle **(Figure 4)**, bring the ends flush together (*they have to touch!*), solder, pickle, polish, marvel at your wonderful craftsmanship, pack it up into a gift box, present to someone special . . . (you get the idea).

Figure 3

Figure 4

Soldering Stone Settings to Your Pieces

We've made some pretty terrific pieces so far, but sometimes you just want to add a little extra "bling" in the form of a gemstone or two.

Fortunately, there are some very clever findings available to make this easy as pie (well, easy, anyway—every time I try to make pie it's a kitchen disaster). A good rule of thumb when adding stone setting findings to your jewelry is to not set the stones until the very last step (pickle, polish, antique, tumble, whatever—all this should be done without stones close by).

We're going to add a prong finding to hold an amethyst (or whatever you choose) and a bezel cup to hold a tiger eye (ditto) to a silver pin decorated with some scrap metal and wire. Then we're going to add a purely practical finding—a pin back—to the back of the piece using the same soldering technique.

Soldering. The technique is the same, no matter what kind of finding you are soldering to the piece. Dab a small circle of flux right where you want your finding to go. Make sure the fluxed area is at least as big as the base of your finding (if the finding extends past the fluxed area, some of the finding may not solder firmly).

Place a small (2mm × 2mm) chip of sheet solder right into the dot of flux. Usually I like to let the flux dry at this point. If you apply heat right away, the water-based flux will begin to boil (which is not a bad thing in itself), and the chip of solder maybe jump around and out of the area you want to solder your finding to. Make sure that the bottom of your finding has flux on it, too.

Heating. Direct your torch's flame right onto the fluxed area with the chip of solder. It is very important that you not remove the flame now until you are done. You may be tempted to remove the flame when the solder melts—DON'T! You may be tempted to remove the flame just as you place the finding down—DON'T! Here's what's going to happen: First the

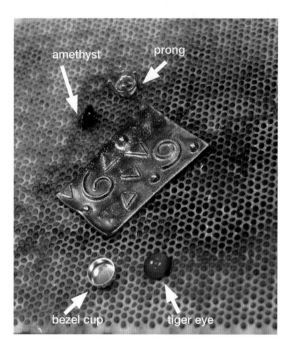

amethyst   prong

bezel cup   tiger eye

Figure 1

solder will melt (when it's hot enough) and turn into a sphere. Next, when the metal gets hot enough for the solder to flow into it (remember the *sub-molecular interstitial bond*?), the solder sphere will turn into a puddle.

Placing the gemstones. Quickly now, pick up your finding with tweezers and place it directly into the puddle of solder and pull it into position **(Figure 1)**. Don't remove the flame yet! (You don't get two tries at this, so get it right while the solder is still molten!)

Figure 2

Figure 3

Figure 4

Once the finding is hot enough, you will see the solder "wick" onto the base of it. Only now should you quickly remove the flame before the finding begins to melt! Stressed out yet? Not to worry. It's easier than it sounds. Repeat steps to adhere the bezel cup **(Figures 2 and 3)**. Here's the basic piece with a prong finding and a bezel cup soldered to it **(Figure 4)**.

Figure 1

Figure 2

Figure 3

Bezel cups. These findings are exactly what they're called, small cups, the sides of which are used to create a bezel. Bezel cups are used to hold flat backed stones (cabochons). Using a tool called a bezel pusher (really little more than a metal post with a big comfy handle), you fold the walls down onto the edges of the cabochon, holding it fast.

After you've soldered a bezel cup in place on your piece, as described on page 91, put the cabochon into the bezel cup **(Figures 1 and 2)**. The bezel wall needs to be only high enough that when it is folded down onto the cabochon, it covers only a very thin area around the perimeter of the stone. Cabochons range from very thin to quite thick. If your stone sits too deep in the bezel cup, you can cut a small circle of sheet metal (or cardboard, paper, whatever) to place under the cabochon, elevating it a little to the right height.

Prong findings. These findings are readily available in most regular cut-stone sizes from 2mm to bigger than is practical for most jewelry!

After you've soldered a prong finding onto your piece, as above, use stone setting tweezers to hold your stone in place while you gently pinch the prongs closed with chain-nose pliers **(Figures 3 and 4)**. (Small notches in the prongs will hold the stone in place.)

Pin backs. These findings are usually sold in sets of three parts: the catch part that holds the pin, the lever base that the pin pivots on, and the pin itself. You can solder the catch and the pivot base as close together as you please, but no farther away from each other than the length of the pin. Once you've soldered the two pieces to the back, place the pin in the catch and cut the pin just past the catch. File the tip of the pin into a sharp point so it will go through fabric without snapping fibers.

Figure 4

Pin back

Rings and Chains

Tools

- Basics (see ** items, pages 13–30)
- Wooden dowel
- Flush-cutter pliers OR
- Saw frame and blade plus masking tape
- Torch, soldering surface, sheet solder, flux

Materials

- Sterling silver wire, 18 gauge

The first technique works well when you need just a few rings or rings of an unusually large size. (Maybe you are making some linked-ring Byzantine chain bracelets!) The second technique is better suited for cranking out a lot of rings of uniform size. (Maybe you're making a chain-mail dress—who knows?)

Making jump rings. Jump rings are simple rings of metal that are used to connect things together, or linked together in myriad patterns to make many different kinds of chains and mail (sheets of linked rings, yeah, like in armor!). Of course you can buy jump rings, but it's often handy to be able to make your own—especially if you want to make an unusual chain or create mail that will require a great many rings. Here are a couple of quick and easy techniques for cutting the rings. The soldering process is the same for either of them.

In either case, start by wrapping wire around a wooden dowel **(Figure 1)**. The size of the dowel will ultimately determine the inside diameter of the rings. Make sure the wraps are nice and tight up against each other—no gaps between wraps **(Figure 2)**.

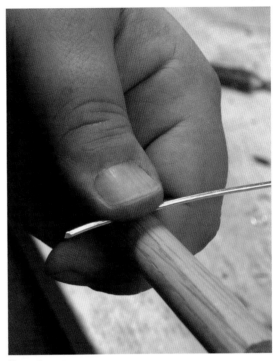

Figure 1

Figure 2

Figure 3

Figure 4

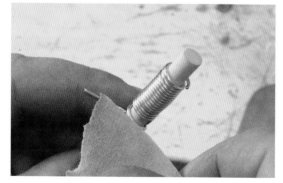

Figure 5

Cutting technique 1. Before you cut the rings, let me bring something about your cutters to your attention. If you close the cutters and have a look at where the cutting blades come together, you will see that at on one side they come together nice and flush. On the other side they come together at the bottom of a deep wedge. When you cut wire with these cutters, the side of the wire that comes off the flush side will have a nice flush end, where the side of the wire that comes off the wedged side will have a pointed bevel on the end of the wire.

You want the joint where your jump rings come together to have two flush ends (so they line up nicely against each other), so you can't just cut willy-nilly down the coil or one side of every ring will have a point to it.

Instead, you need to make two cuts for every jump ring. The first cut uses the flush side of your cutters to "clean" off the end of the coil **(Figure 3)**. You then must turn your pliers around so the flush side of the cutters face the opposite direction so when you cut the other end of this ring off, it will also be flush.

If you look at the end of the coil now, there will be a point on the end—so you need to turn your cutters around again to clean the end off, and turn them around yet again to cut the ring off, and so on for each ring **(Figure 4)**.

Cutting technique 2. After you've wrapped wire around the dowel, tape the coil tightly to the dowel with masking tape, covering the coil completely **(Figure 5)**.

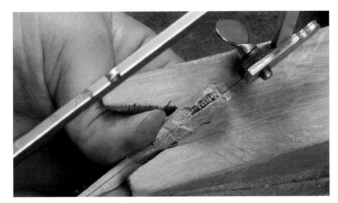

Figure 6

Holding the end of the dowel in your bench pin, begin sawing down the side of the coil, keeping the saw blade in line with the dowel **(Figure 6)**. Don't try to cut too many rings at once. Keep the saw blade angled so you are only cutting through three or four rings at a time. Yes, you are meant to be sawing into the dowel.

Once the whole coil has been sawn through, you can get your saw blade out by releasing the blade from the far end of the saw and pulling down as though you are sawing more **(Figure 7)**. Your blade should slide easily out without snapping.

Now you can peel open the masking tape (like a tamale), and all those gorgeous jump rings will slide off the end of the dowel **(Figure 8)**.

If you have access to a tumbler, by all means use it to tumble-burnish rings cut this way, because they sometimes have small burrs along the cut edges that will snag fabric. Polishing these off by hand is possible but tedious.

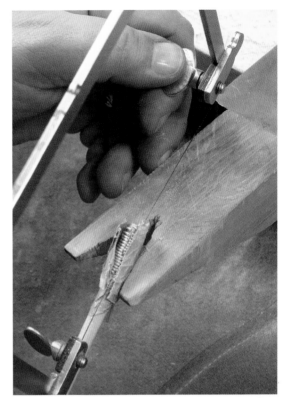

Figure 7

Figure 8

Figure 1

Figure 2

Figure 3

Soldering jump rings. This blow-by-blow may seem really short, but the truth is there is not much to it. After you've soldered a bunch of rings, it will be second nature.

Make sure the ends of each ring are a) clean, and b) tight fitting, touching each other. Flux the areas in and around the joint to be soldered **(Figure 1)**. Cut off a small piece of clean solder and lay it on the soldering board. With your torch, melt the piece of solder into a molten sphere. As soon as it forms a ball, scoop it up with your soldering pick **(Figure 2)**.

Begin slowly heating the ring until it takes on a warm peachy glow that indicates the proper temperature **(Figure 3)**. Just as the temperature is reached, place the ball of solder right in between the two cut ends of the ring, keeping the flame on the piece the whole time. When the piece is hot enough, the solder will "flow" into the joint, virtually disappearing. Immediately remove the heat, and quench your piece in water. Place it in the pickling bath for cleaning.

Getting Started Making Metal Jewelry

Fused Chain

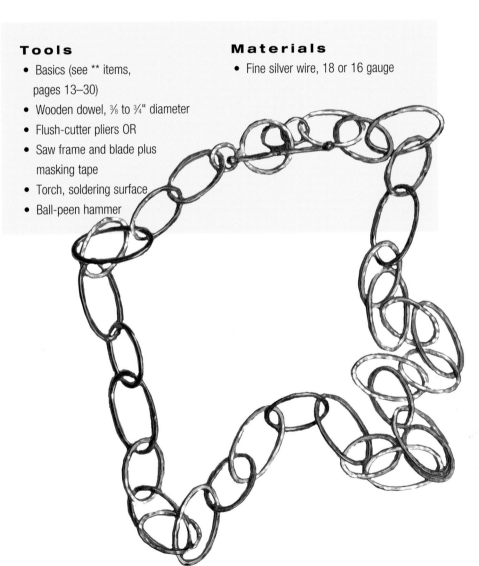

Tools

- Basics (see ** items, pages 13–30)
- Wooden dowel, ⅜ to ¾" diameter
- Flush-cutter pliers OR
- Saw frame and blade plus masking tape
- Torch, soldering surface
- Ball-peen hammer

Materials

- Fine silver wire, 18 or 16 gauge

Chain links can also be fused instead of soldered (with considerably less mess involved). The links in this chain are about 16" in diameter, and I've hammered them into flattened, irregular shapes for a one-of-a-kind look.

The basics of fusing have already been explained in detail on page 37, but there's another consideration when fusing chain links.

Using fine silver vs sterling and soldering. When fusing links for chain, you should use only fine (.999) silver. The reason for this is simple: sterling silver is an alloy that contains copper, which means you'd have to use flux to keep cupric oxides from forming while you are fusing. Fine silver is (arguably) pure, so there is no copper and no need for any other messy chemical agent besides heat (not that heat is a messy chemical agent, but you know what I mean).

Making the chain. Make links the same way you made the jump rings on page 96, around a wooden dowel. Remember to leave two flush ends when cutting the rings.

Before fusing, make sure the ends are tight up against each other. They must be touching in order for the fusing to work. Basically this is a little like two drops of water on a car windshield. When the two drops meet each other, they quickly join together and "fuse" into one drop.

The challenge is that if you get the ring too hot and too molten, then ends will begin to pull away from each other, ultimately separating and forming two separate spheres. You need to heat the joint just enough that both sides to be joined enter the liquidus range around the same time and merge (fuse, like the drops of water) before it all gets too molten. It might be best to do this in a low, romantically lit setting, as it's easier to see the glowing metal change.

Practice a few times with single, loose rings. While your torch is directed at the joint in the ring, the heat is dissipating along the rest of the ring, radiating out away from it and keeping it (relatively) cool. Try to keep the flame aimed at the joint so that heat buildup will overwhelm the dissipative properties of the metal and reach flow temperature. This sounds complicated, but it will make sense as you do it.

Fusing and quenching. Place a link on the soldering board, and begin heating the area around the joint with your torch **(Figure 1)**. The link will begin to change color, eventually acquiring a very faint, dull orange glow. Just past this temperature, you will see the surface begin to shimmer and become very shiny—this is the "liquidus" range! At this point, the molten ends will fuse together (like the raindrops in the car window), and you must quickly pull the torch away before the whole thing begins to melt.

Quench the link in water. It will be cool enough to handle in just a moment. Now you can add another link (and another, and so on, until your chain is complete).

Figure 1

Figure 2

Attaching links. When you attach the next link and are preparing to fuse it closed, hang the previously fused ones off the side of your soldering board and turn the opening to be fused as far away from the other loops as possible **(Figure 2)**. This will ensure that you are able to fuse the area around the joint, but not fuse the links to each other!

Hammering/hardening the links. Once you've fused all the links together, you can stretch them, bend them, twist them or fold them into whatever shape you want. You can elongate a link by inserting round-nose pliers in the link and stretching them open **(Figure 3)**.

One technique I like to use is a very random hammering of the links with the ball side of my ball-peen hammer. Many frequent, lighter taps work better than bashing with all your might—you may end up with some too-thin areas if you hit the links too hard.

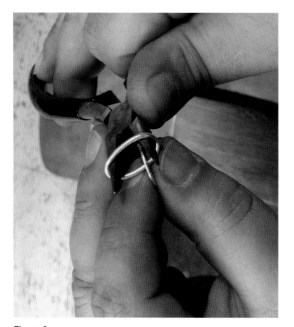

Figure 3

Place only as much of the loop as is possible (while keeping the loop flat) on your bench block, hanging the remainder of the loop (and the rest of the chain) off the side **(Figure 4)**. Carefully hammer all around this section of the link.

Once you've done that half, rotate the link around so the unhammered areas are accessible for hammering.

The other side. After completing one side, you will have to turn the loop over and hammer the other side as well, so you have some nice texture on both sides of the loop **(Figure 5)**. Be especially careful to only use very light taps on this side, lest you flatten out the other side and you'll have to start the whole thing over!

Just keep doing this for every link in the chain, and in no time you'll have a hammered-loop fused chain everyone will envy!

Figure 4

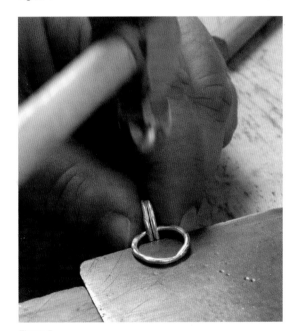

Figure 5

AND FINALLY . . .

You've worked through all the projects in this book, at least once. You understand all the fundamental processes involved in making metal jewelry—how to do them, how they work. You may still be a little slow, you may make a few missteps, but you've got the basics. You can look at almost any piece of jewelry and think, "Hey, I could do that!"

You're on your way to a world of creativity. If you can imagine it, now you can truly do it.

Suppliers and Resources

The Bead Factory Inc.
3019 6th Ave.
Tacoma, WA 98406
Toll-free: (888) 500-BEAD
www.TheBeadFactory.com

Specializing in higher quality beads, findings, tools, and supplies, The Bead Factory carries everything from basic Czech glass to diamond strands. The Bead Factory is your direct source for quality beading supplies, tools, pliers, wire, books, stringing materials, miracle beads, and kits. They feature their own exclusive Wiremaster line of pliers and wire. The Bead Factory also has an extensive selection of workshops. They have classes every day in various beading techniques, including wirework, seed-beading, PMC, stringing, metalsmithing, glass bead making, soldering, and the jewelry business.

Baubles & Beads
1676 Shattuck Ave.
Berkeley, CA 94709
(510) 644-BEAD
www.baublesandbeads.com

1104 4th St.
San Rafael, CA 94901
(415) 457-8891
www.baublesandbeads.com

Baubles & Beads has the best in beads, supplies, books, local teachers, and nationally known guest instructors. If you are just getting started with beads or want more challenges in metal, wire or PMC, Baubles & Beads has great classes for you! Your source for bead, classes, books, and tools in Berkeley and San Rafael.

Beadissimo
1051 Valencia
San Francisco, CA 94110
(415) 282-BEAD
www.beadissimo.com

Carrying a wide selection of beads, clasps, finding, and tools. Beadissimo is dedicated to promoting creativity and individuality. Their expert staff provides interesting and unique products to help anyone interested in designing and creating jewelry achieve a sense of accomplishment and satisfaction.

Rio Grande
7500 Bluewater Rd. NW
Albuquerque, NM 87121
(800) 545-6566
www.riogrande.com

Rio Grande is a supplier to people who make or sell jewelry. Their distribution lines—tools, equipment, gems, findings, displays, and packaging—are known worldwide. Rio Grande remains an industry leader, highly respected for serving customers with integrity and high standards in jewelry manufacture and distribution.

Books of Interest

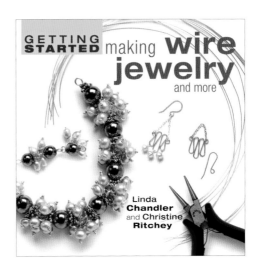

All Wired Up

Create findings, ear wires, clasps, and cages using the detailed instructions and step-by-step instructions in this best-selling book.

Paperbound, 8½ × 9, 128 pages, $21.95

Getting Started Making Wire Jewelry

Winner of the Benjamin Franklin Best Craft Book of 2006! No prior wireworking knowledge needed. *Getting Started Making Wire Jewelry* walks you, step by step, through the entire process from shopping for wire to gauge to tools.

Paper over board, 8 × 8, 96 pages, $16.95

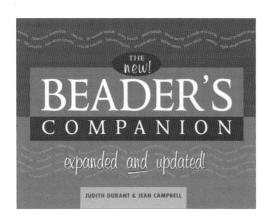

The New Beader's Companion

Still chock-full of definitions, illustrations, and techniques but completely revamped, including color photographs and a new section on semi-precious stone beads.

Hardbound, semi-concealed wire-o binding, 7 × 5, 128 pages, $19.95

Findings and Finishings

This invaluable guide describes how to use purchased findings as well as new ways to create your own. Also included are innovative finishing techniques for necklaces, bracelets, earrings, and more!

Paperbound, 8½ × 9, 128 pages, $21.95

About the Author

Mark Lareau started his wireworking and metalsmithing odyssey in 1998 when he began making simple wire jewelry and basic mobiles. In 1992, Mark and his wife, Viki, opened The Bead Factory, a full-service retail bead store in Tacoma, Washington, and he has been teaching classes there ever since. Viki and Mark are also the founders of the Puget Sound Bead Festival, the most successful consumer bead event on the West Coast. Mark is the author of *All Wired Up* (Interweave Press, 2000), with 75,000 copies sold.

Index